"*Refuge* is that rare memoir, a highly intimate story with global reverberations. Ming Holden's sensitive and openhearted account of her encounters with refugees all over the world challenged assumptions, both personal and political, that I didn't know I had. This book aches with radical compassion, shines with easy wit, stuns with frank truth, and sings with miraculous beauty. I read it with astonishment, and walked away from it a better citizen."

RACHEL LYON, author of *Self-Portrait With Boy*

"Evocative, penetratingly intelligent, and propelled by a fierce and tender sense of empathy, Ming Holden's writing dwells close to the living, beating heart of her material. Read this compelling and thought-provoking collection of essays if you want to be challenged, enervated, inspired, and astonished."

ALEXANDRA KLEEMAN, author of *You Too Can Have A Body Like Mine*

"In *Refuge*, we have an entertaining and edgy travelogue of a woman in a world of geo-political social structures. Ming Holden's unique existential framework gets up close: focused and humorous, and then wide, keen and surprising. This double-vision allows the reader the pleasure of a landscape made of inner and outer worlds scanned by weird beams of consciousness: observed and observing, immersed and removed, intimate and foreign."

THALIA FIELD, author of *Point and Line*

"Ming Holden is living an extraordinary life. These stories weave its many strands together in evocative, tender, and sometimes heartbreaking ways."

ANNE-MARIE SLAUGHTER, President & CEO, New America

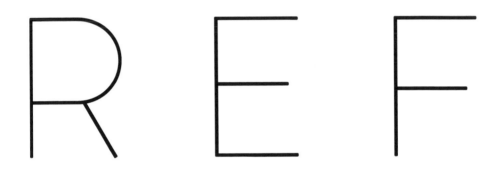

REF

A MEMOIR

KORE PRESS TUCSON 2018

MING HOLDEN

UGE

Celebrating 25 Years!
Standing by women's words since 1993
Kore Press, Inc., Tucson, Arizona USA
www.korepress.org

Cover photograph by Julie Poncet
Design and layout by James Meetze

We express gratitude to the the Arts Foundation for Tucson and Southern Arizona, the Arizona Commission on the Arts, and to individuals for support to make this Kore Press publication possible.

ISBN 978-1-888553-95-6

Library of Congress Cataloging-in-Publication Data

Names: Holden, Ming, author.
Title: Refuge : a memoir / Ming Lauren Holden.
Description: Tucson : Kore Press, 2018. | Includes bibliographical references
   and index.
Identifiers: LCCN 2018002478 | ISBN 9781888553956 (trade book : alk. paper)
Subjects: LCSH: Holden, Ming. | Women authors--Biography. | International
   travel--Anecdotes. | Arts in social service. | Self-actualization
   (Psychology)
Classification: LCC PS3608.O48323 A46 2018 | DDC 818/.603--dc23
LC record available at https://lccn.loc.gov/2018002478

for my father

CONTENTS

Rhode Island, USA

ROSE

I am accustomed, now, to being in a room with seven men who are drawing my pubic hair. I have been on the other side of the drawing board, and I know that bodies are reduced to shape, distance, and shadow: hold up the pencil. This is how far the nipple is from the armpit. Squint. It is not even a nipple anymore, not to them, though my nipple has not changed any since I took off my clothing.

The first time I posed naked in the basement of the man whose ad I answered, there were only two artists. The host would grimace and then relax his face in quick succession like a broken smile doll while he sketched. The other rubbed my shoulders over the thick blue robe during a break. The music was incredible: blues, and old music from 1940's Japan. Bad luck for the band, my host comments, because then Hiroshima happened. I found something to focus on so my body would hold still and steady. One time it was a finished drawing. Something about the light on the woman's breast made it look like the shape bread dough takes before rising. When I arrived I asked for the bathroom. Perhaps because I come from a place where basements and attics are rare I love them, and his basement smelled pleasant and damp, pastel and cardboard everywhere, with a cat who wound round the artist's legs. But the kitchen and bathroom betrayed the smell of the five cats total who live there. At my family home we have five cats also, but they spend their time outside accruing foxtails. The wife had headphones on and didn't look at me as she hurried into the car he had taken to pick me up from campus. He spoke to her as if he didn't know she had tuned him out. I stood bare under the hot lamp unsure of whether I was welcome, holding onto the curtain so my arm would catch the light, staring into the face of the clock until it became an object representative of nothing important, bread, an elbow, skin, scattered records. I do not know why there are no women in this group. I wonder sometimes if I would feel differently about shedding my clothing for a woman. I do not think I would; though I am using my naked body in a way a man dictates, I have sanctioned this and am making forty dollars in three hours. I also love the bluegrass, I love lying down during breaks and reading essays and books for my courses, I love the corner with all of the records and pastels strewn like pick-up sticks.

They are drawing my person but it is not personal. If it were not my body, but another's, they would still be gauging, squinting, marking. The only time the fact of their masculinity becomes acute to me is when it occurs to me that I know as little of their minds as they know of mine, that any or all could have committed a rape twenty years back, or two days back. I do not fear for my safety. I only would rather they not see me when I slide the robe off and hang it over the chair: that is the one moment that feels intimate.

How are you, one of the irregular comers asks the man who leads and hosts the drawing group. I'm okay, he says, in the kind of way that suggests both men know he has recently not been so okay. This man, who teaches at a nearby art school and whose figure drawings sell, tells me which way to roll my hips and whether to expose my ear, but I have no right to ask about these other things, just as I have no right to sneak a dried apricot or two or a vanilla cookie from his kitchen when I take my bathroom break, though I do just that.

I do not know where the wife goes. She does not always leave the house. I think she stays upstairs. There is sometimes a cat on the stairs, a calico one. There is almost always a homemade baked good on the counter. I never touch that, the pie or cobbler, though I wonder whether it is he or she who bakes them. Lately their daughter, who is a year younger than I, has been stashing her boxes in the living room while she moves from her apartment to an art collective. I have never met the daughter; I have only heard about her artwork and music projects from her father, who is very proud. I like to ask him about his only child and prompt him to say something politically leftist. This is how to get him going. The only two ways I know and can use, and want to use, to get him going.

At the end of the evening sessions there has started to be that clarity of star winking above the deck, a bite to the air, to the shadow of roof: autumn. At the end of an afternoon session I straighten my jacket on the deck, scoop-shaped yellow leaves heaping all over the deck and deck chair, and turn to smile at the men filing out, saddled with art supplies. Take care, they tell me.

II.

The first broken heart I ever had I woke up feeling like ropes were tying me
to the bed, crisscrossing plushly but firmly, and I could not move my body
under their weight, and my mind did not want my body to move under
their weight. That was also the way it felt when I woke up after election day,
2004. Certain thoughts I have make me a political leftist. The thoughts have
a lot to do with my body, actually, and its landscape of hip and skin being
one over which I, my thoughts, preside. I read the results of the election and
I floated on my bed, floated and was also tied there: I could not nudge my
thoughts or my body and so they could not nudge each other, either. And
when I talked the next day to a dear friend who devoted her vacation time to
liberal activism, she had a hollowness to her voice, and described it like this: it
feels like I have had a break up, it feels like someone has died. Neither of us
could move either our thoughts or our bodies in ourselves or in each other,
but it was a lucky feeling to not nudge together, to not be able to nudge
together. I remember to think sometimes, in the middle of the twenty
minutes between breaks, the muscles in my calf or neck or arm starting to
ache, the tiny muscles I did not know were there and certainly have never
used for this long continuously, that these men have traveled, been married,
probably been divorced, probably been discovered masturbating by their
mothers, perhaps discovered their own sons masturbating, perhaps raise
their voices when they are angry, like cream in their coffee, do not like
cream in their coffee, prefer Toyotas to Acuras and rain to sun, hate their
job, love their job, remember that year they spent hating their first out-of-
college job in Phoenix, regret smoking so much weed or starting to smoke
cigarettes, miss their grandmother Doris who smelled like rice pilaf. One
thing I realize now that I have not done is use my brain time while I hold
my body still to invent histories for them—for instance, the man with the
Cape Cod shirt might be a lawyer with two kids and a secret love for reality
television. The man with the sexy eyes whose eyes make me uncomfortable
because I think they are sexy has traveled in South America. I do not do
that. Rather, I daydream about writing and sleeping with my new Boy, I
remember other Boys, I try not to cry when the Patti Griffin song about
rain comes on, I worry about what I will do with my self to earn money
over the summer. I forget the men are there.

It does occur to me that it is the right of any person to say I do not want to be naked anymore in front of you and step down from under the bright lights, and that were I to do that nothing more than losing this job would come of it whereas over history this may not have always been the case. I have never needed to do things with my naked body that I did not want to do, as is my right, and for which I also feel guilty since most women I know have had that right taken away from them at one or many points.

Slavery, also, has been described as not owning one's life; in other words, not owning one's body. Since we can think whatever we like and not say it, for one's life to be controlled is then the control of the body, which is trackable and seeable in ways our thoughts are not. We can even use our bodies to say exactly different things from what our minds are thinking, like I hate you when we are thinking I love you, or the other way around. I cannot tell if one of these happens more than the other. They both seem to happen a lot. Sometimes my fingers fall asleep from holding onto the blanket hung from the ceiling, but the artists need the arm upraised so I keep the fingers there and rub them when the clock's wide face looks roundly up at me with the right whiskers and then I move.

III.

There is a red rose on my desk that has been opening since Friday. It is Sunday. On Friday my new Boy's only very recently ex-girlfriend came into town for a tournament between universities. I have not met her. At 3 a.m. Friday morning my new Boy bought me the rose in a Providence Seven Eleven. My new Boy is not actually mine; I do not own him. The rose is in the only thing that I could find to serve as a vase at 4 a.m. on a Friday morning in a dirty apartment shared with three guys: a washed-out forty-ounce beer bottle. The rose has done quite well, blooming an aching red on my white desk next to my printer (though the desk is not mine either, it belongs to the university) and I have somehow attached my hope that the Boy will still want to hold my body and call it his—in the nice way that we can lay claim to one another's bodies sometimes—to the rose and how well it has done over the weekend we agreed he would be sorting things out with the ex. Now on Sunday evening one petal, full and triangular and on the lower left end of the blossom from where I am sitting, looks like it might drop from the flower soon. There is only a faint smell, but even during more difficult moments this weekend when I have thought in my mind of punitive things to say to the Boy if things do not go as I would like, I have touched my nose to this, this cracking-open red star, and pushed my face into a smile to get my mind to follow. There is a thought in me that would like to hold the ex's hand and explain that I did not expect this, and there is a thought in me that suspects she will not be the ex after all, and I will be the one to be sad. The verdict has not happened yet to nudge my body into reflecting one or the other of these thoughts, or even a third or fourth or fifth thought that is different from the first two. I have never met someone who had to change something with someone else to make room for me, and I am not used to being the Woman in Red.

I walk into the kitchen where there is a poster of Andy Warhol. The one with two of the same picture, two of his faces ringed by a tambourine. Paul's pressed leaves are on the hall wall. The floor is littered with trash. Take care, meaning, take care of yourself. And the self that takes care of me, the me that is different from the self that does the caring for, are these two different parts of me, even, from the me that does the thinking and the me whose shapes and breasts and thighs seven men just spent hours drawing?

Even to owe something to oneself is a schizophrenic term, someone told me once. To do anything to oneself. There is I, there is I doing something to myself, to my self. I think now that our language just does not know what to do with this: if someone cuts their own wrist, then the giver and receiver of the action are the same. Why isn't it my self is doing this to my self? I am doing it to me? But no, the correct way to say it is that I am doing something to my self, and so I am a different entity from my self.

Sometimes, on break, I hold my breath through the kitchen that smells like cat pee to the bathroom and take off the robe and look. I take off the robe and look at what they have been drawing; it is strange that they know better the shapes of my shoulders than I do, strange that I forgot about the tattoo on the back they have been drawing and on which they must have seen the tattoo. There is a *New Yorker* Cartoon on the wall: "I'd invite you in, but my life is a mess." The first time someone broke my heart I wrote that the act of love is also one of impaling. A lost event. A poltergeist. I cannot clean places I cannot reach, I wrote. Up in front of all of those grown men, on display, I do not feel vulnerable.

IV.

I pause while reading an essay about holocausts and crimes against humanity suffered by Jews in different countries and Japanese-Americans in this country and other groups in other countries because my roommate Brian has enlisted me to help with a very short film for his media class. I am to act. I am glad to, because I need a break from the part of myself that is trying to gather up feeling good about anything after the election and an essay that is about what this one is about. I need a break from the part of myself that looks at the rose every few minutes. I need a break from the part of myself that is imagining all of the bodies in Sudan and Rwanda and back centuries in the Ottoman Empire and back decades in Germany. I need a break from the part of myself that knows that as many memories and dreams were attached to the bodies as are attached to me, only memories and dreams are not attached anymore to those bodies and they are to mine. I need a break from the part of myself that thumps painfully whenever the part of myself that looks at the rose every few minutes looks at the rose every few minutes.

It is my first autumn in Providence and the leaves, which are tawny and shaped like boats, and the breeze, which is warm and full-smelling, make me glad. I have a cigarette partly because my character is to smoke one and partly because I have had only four cigarettes in six months and would like another. Another thing that makes me glad is that my character does things I like to do or would like to do: walk through fall leaves, see newspapers detailing Bush's victory, set them on fire, let them burn for a moment, stamp out the flames, walk away (again through the fall leaves, which is my favorite part because I like fall leaves a lot), take out a journal, write in it furiously, look at the camera, take a drag, and smile. It was Brian who went to New Hampshire, into the projects, on election day, and Brian who decided on Wednesday to be nicer to everyone than he had been during the preceding weeks and think of people primarily as systems of family and friends and not as participants in the body politic. My roommates and I know about and read about and talk about the body—and by the body I mean the bodies we

19

use to get too drunk and make love and have sex (which are different things, even we know) and get our selves to classes, and by the body I also mean the big body whose disconnect I feel in this, my small body, when I cannot nudge this, my small body; I mean the big body that is the body politic.

Jake sits on the curb in his beret and moccasins and watches, waiting to help Brian move the dolly. I crouch in the street and wait with the matchbook. I do not know what Brian thinks, or Jake, or the Boy. I do know that I love them all, Brian and Jake, and the Boy, as I crouch in my jacket with my hair on my face and matches in my hands. I know also that in some way I love the seven men who have drawn my pubic hair, not because they have drawn my pubic hair but because the room is quiet save for the bluegrass music playing while they draw and I stand still, and there is buzzing and whirring inside them that I cannot hear, and memories inside them that I cannot see.

Atmeh, Syria
&
Reyhanli, Turkey
&
California, USA

THE SUREST WAY
TO SURVIVE

First, there's the warm air. Then the strong sunlight. Then the quiet balcony, shading a long white plastic table. Then the shapes and colors of the food: bright red cuts of tomato, cucumber, hummus, dark shiny olives. Then the garden outside, a modest plot with hopeful green stalks.

A block away, next to a paved road, rises a hill. The hill is a summer sort of light-brown.

Shuffling and murmuring. Bread coming in wide discs and torn off by hand. Then the hands doing the tearing, some young, some scarred, some old. A handsome young man sits to my right, with a smile like my old childhood friend Tristan. He laughs at me trying to fit too much into my mouth at once. A quiet man with white hair leans back, looking at his hands grasped in his lap. Four more guys in their late twenties dig in, pouring Coke for everybody and passing plates, conversing quietly in Arabic. The silence presses in, as though the sunlight itself enforced it. When it isn't very windy, it's very still. A cat noses the crumbling sidewalk below, near a pile of plaster limbs.

Only now do I feed myself another bit of the story. The man my age who looks and grins like Tristan and who asks for a picture with me, adjusts his torso in his wheelchair. He shakes the stump coming from his hip as though he usually tapped his foot, as though it were a habit of his, before his legs were blown off by one of Assad's shells. His hands are that graceful because he was a barber, standing in front of his shop when the shell hit eight months ago.

The quiet, white haired man? Give him eight years in a cell in the 80s. Add that history to him, unseen and unverified.

And make the hill a few hundred feet off, the one that looks like it could be California wine country: draw a border, an invisible border, halfway up the hill, and call the country beyond Syria.

*

I am in Reyhanli, a tiny town in Turkey right on the Syrian border that only became internationally well-known when three bombs went off here in a coordinated attack in May 2013. Because it is meters from the border, Reyhanli has doubled in population. The man who sold me the green patterned dress I am wearing crawled the last of the way through sewage pipes to Reyhanli from Syria. His shop is not far from the seedy hotel where wealthy Gulf country donors come to meet and pass along funds to Free Syrian Army agents.

Abu Faisal, the man who offered to take me into Syria, asks me to lock the metal bar above our knees into place, securing us in our seats as best as we can be secured. Across from us his cousin, Abu Abdo Al Halabi (recognizable by his serious unibrow) does the same in the seat he shares with a surgeon who fled Damascus after being forced to treat six of Assad's soldiers at gunpoint.

The engine clanks to life and my heart begins racing. It thumps harder when the huge contraption of metal and tires under us begins to move through the evening breeze.

"I've never done this before," I breathe to Abu Faisal, though I suspect that's obvious. I grip the bar and look around, wondering what to focus on so I don't get more sick as we pick up speed.

"Looks like I chose the wrong night to wear a dress," I say. Abu Faisal chuckles.

I tuck the fabric on either side of my thighs as best I can, then let out an involuntary whoop as the ride picks up speed, rocking us up and down through the air, above the game booths and the children's car carousel and the pepper trees shuddering in the wind.

*

Dr. Mahrouz spent around six months with Bashar Assad a few decades back when they were both in medical programs, smoking and playing cards. "Med school?" I ask when Dr. Mahrouz tells me this. "Assad's a doctor?"

"An ophthalmologist!" he says. "How did you not know Assad is an ophthalmologist? You know nothing."

"I don't know anything," I agree. "I'm not a journalist. I haven't researched much."

The quiet older man to my left, who was part of the Muslim Brotherhood before becoming disillusioned with it in the 80s and spending nearly a decade in jail, says something to Dr. Mahrouz, who translates: "He is saying you should cover up in the camp."

"I brought scarves and long sleeves," I say. "I didn't think I needed to wear them today. Would you prefer I put them on?"

"No, no, we don't mind," says Dr. Mahrouz. "In fact we are thoroughly enjoying it."

Dr. Mahrouz, a Syrian cardiologist based in the U.K., has never met a vegetable he doesn't like. He keeps dashing off when we're walking to or from dinner in Reyhanli to buy or uproot one (or three). He tells me that our motley crew's Muslim guys are lucky I don't understand Arabic. He explains the Muslim afterlife thusly: "A river of wine! So many women, and the ugliest one is more beautiful than Angelina Jolie!"

Dr. Mahrouz goes into Syria once every one or two months to deliver aid. His mother still lives in his village of Maarrat al-Nu'man. He and his brother Ahmed, who is the commander of Maarrat's Free Syrian Army unit, are carrying the village on their shoulders. Today in the upstairs portion of a prosthetic limb center in Reyhanli, where the families of amputees stay while their loved ones are fitted and rehabilitated and where we are all sleeping, Dr. Mahrouz hands me a passport-size photo of himself in uniform. In it his hair is darker, but he has remained handsome even in his middle age. The problem is, he knows it. When he hears I am undecided about crossing the border into Syria, he sits next to me and lowers his voice to a suggestive level.

"You know," he purrs, "once you go into the camp you might realize that you like it and are not as afraid as you might think. The feeling when you go further into Syria, with everything happening, can be... well, it can be exciting."

He raises an eyebrow, smirking. For perhaps the first and only time, he's actually waiting for me to talk.

I'm a creative writer and not a journalist, with no conflict zone experience and none of the street smarts required for it. I have no poker face and all the diplomatic discretion of Honey-Boo-Boo. Even to cross the border about twenty meters into Atmeh "Olive Tree" refugee camp is a technically illegal move, and as America cut diplomatic ties with Syria, my government could do nothing for me if I were captured. Even to cross the border at all is, technically, to enter a war zone.

Outside, the voices of children, slow shifting of stalks. The glass of tea in my hand is translucent and amber, shaped like a woman. An hourglass.

"I'll think about it," I tell Dr. Mahrouz.

II.

In the office/spare room of my cousin Cliff's house in Oakland, California, the woman with the eyes is there, watching me as I sleep, watching me like a hawk. She watches over the wonderful guest bed, the bed that has a memory foam mattress and is covered in Siamese kitty hair (and sometimes the kitties themselves, if I am lucky). I have woken up by the woman with the eyes in Cliff's house at least once a year for a decade now; I first visited him and his partner Dorothy when I was eighteen, after my first semester of college. These visits to them became a mainstay. I watched their lives arc through engagement to marriage to child number one and child number two; I helped them move from a little house in the Castro to a slightly larger one in Oakland; I watched Cliff's garden grow a little bigger every year, the wee greenhouse pungent with tomato plants. Their children, Penelope and Max, are the first ones I've known well since they were born as I myself am the last cousin in my generation to come along. Penelope, who is six, is a big-emotion-haver and also brilliant at everything from backflips to thousand-piece Lego sets; her little brother Max, who's four, is a mellow dude with a wicked sense of humor and a perfect accent when he pronounces Spanish words. Their parents met in college and feed them food from Trader Joe's and work excessively as engineer and consultant to give their children what all children deserve.

You've probably seen the woman with the eyes, who has been made an example of. Her eyes are green. There's a rust-colored headscarf lightly wrapped around her head but not covering so much that we can't see her brown hair. The photo of the woman with the eyes, known generally as "The Afghan Girl," has always been in the guest room, since 2002 when I started visiting Cliff and Dorothy. It's framed and I remember Dorothy once called her "stunning," which about summed it up.

If one day I returned and the photo had gone, I would miss it. I can't remember if I saw the photo before that, but I saw it years after, in a lesson plan in graduate school. We were to show it to our elementary composition students for their photo analysis lesson. The woman with the eyes was the example of "demand." There is offer, and there is demand. If the subject is staring at the camera, the subject is demanding something.

The photo was taken in Pakistan in 1984 by Steve McCurry. There was "a haunted look" in the girl's eyes, McCurry would say later, so he got her permission to photograph her. She was twelve or so. She'd made the two-week trek to Nasir Bagh refugee camp on the Afghanistan-Pakistan border after the Soviet invasion that killed her parents. She had come with her siblings around the age of six here on a trek that was often itself a fatal journey. It was snowy and they would beg for blankets, hiding in caves if jets came. Her haunted look seemed representative of her struggle and that of the refugees McCurry saw in the camp. His photograph of her became the most recognizable one in the history of the *National Geographic* and letters arrived in a stream over the next seventeen years. Some people committed to work in Pakistan in refugee camps because of that photo. People wanted to adopt her. Sponsor her. Marry her.

The photo was used on promotional Amnesty International materials during those seventeen years. It is so iconic as to feature on the cover of the commemorative "Special Members Edition" of *National Geographic*. The young woman herself had no idea, for almost twenty years, that she was famous. She didn't see the picture until 2002. (Perhaps she is not a Special Member.)

By 2002, when she saw the only photo ever taken of herself, she had borne four daughters, not all of whom survived. She had been called the Mona Lisa of the Twentieth Century.

But her name isn't Mona Lisa. It's Sharbat.

*

This is all to say that in the Atmeh "Olive Tree" Camp, in Syria, there was a girl.

*

In her poem "Trillium," Louise Gluck wrote: *I knew nothing; I could do nothing but see.* As we crossed the border into Syria, I remembered those lines, which seem to me like birth, like what babies experience. If I had known nothing of the violence erupting unpredictably nearby that had brought these people here, to a baking-hot day in July, the children hoping for photos and candy, the men with arresting sea-green eyes and dirt-tinted skin: would I have sensed war and tension? I felt nervous, thought "war zone," made an association that was not based on my experience at all, nothing I could see.

Atmeh "Olive Tree" camp is about fifty meters over the Turkish border into Syria. The olive trees are such a bleached, dusty green, like original Wrigley's chewing gum, that the whole scene is whitewashed—the pale clouds and pale sky and pale trees and pale grayish makeshift tents of a city of 25,000 people who weren't here a year or two ago. In it live some of the poorest Syrians, but the luckiest of the poorest: the ones who could get out of Damascus, Aleppo, Homs.

And yet they are the unluckiest of the lucky: unable to afford paper documentation, they cannot legally get over the border because by the end of 2011 Turkey had closed its borders to paperless refugees. Atmeh camp has yet to be shelled, but Assad's jets did fly overhead late last year.

"Olive tree" because there are olive trees in every direction—and for me they are what make this land different from the land I came from, wine country in central California, because the olive trees are different than the oaks when nothing else is different about the land, not the color of the grass nor its dry-oatweed smell.

As Atmeh camp is on the Syrian side of the border, its United Nations High Commissioner of Refugees (UNHCR)-emblem-stamped tents are kind of contraband. The UNHCR can't enter Syria except at the request of Assad. Assad doesn't want to shelter these people, he wants to kill them. When Angelina Jolie visited Syrian refugees as an official UNHCR envoy, she visited them in Jordan. So did John Kerry. The tents that Maram Foundation founder Yakzan, who tours the camp with us, secured for the camp he had to secure by creating the Maram Foundation in the first place, then receiving the tents in Turkey via a network of other aid agencies, ultimately bringing them over the border himself.

The tents, the ones with blue UNHCR-stamped emblems, are what constitute the classrooms of the makeshift camp school, like the makeshift camp school in which McCurry found twelve-year-old Sharbat with the haunted look in her eyes that came to symbolize the plight of the refugee.

He didn't describe her as "demanding." She was, in fact, shy, and so he approached her last, there in the school tent.

The universal blue UNHCR emblem stamping the contraband tents looks like this: a person shielded by two hands. And around this, the person and hands, a ring of olive tree branches.

*

What I mean to say is that the girl, who was the most beautiful girl, carried a candy bar next to me in the heat for two hours as we toured the camp. I stole glances at her often, beside me. Thick brows, brown skin, brown hair, deep brown eyes, pointed chin. Her face might be the most gorgeous face I've seen on someone her age—she's probably not older than six or seven, around Penelope's age. But she's not cute, she's gorgeous. Like the models on Fashion TV. She wanted me to buy the candy bar. I didn't. I could have. More children would have come, perhaps started to fight. It happened when Dr. Mahrouz gave them chocolate.

We spoke with some of the young people at the school. Their faces were expressive, mischievous, shy. They wanted to practice English. They wanted to know why we weren't Muslim. The littlest children sang for us. Deeper into the country, on bombed-out streets, their peers roam the streets in their third, fourth, fifth, sixth year without schooling. More and more of them were joining various military factions (read: any people with weapons) that dissolved and attributed loyalty to whoever could pay them a salary and decisively arm them, chiefly wealthy private donors from the gulf countries (read: very religious). Family dead, danger, bombs, nightmares daily, broken promises, no routine: phenomenally damaged nervous systems affecting for the worse the lifelong ability to settle down, to sleep, to digest, to think things through, to be functional citizens—of any nation—in any way.

This bleak future is settling in as though it is an inevitability. It is not, but to admit that I must admit how I take painkillers for my headache after the day in the sun, after seeing her and enjoying her gorgeous face as I refused her a coin, after I take a long hot shower and wash the dust of a place with no sewage system off of my shoes.

Words like "suffering," we say in writing workshop, stand in for something else. Go for an arresting image, we advise each other, like the picture of the refugee woman on the cover of *National Geographic,* who is not offering, she's demanding. I will not forget the girl I gave no money to. I did not ask her name. I did not take her picture. Her life is too likely not to benefit from how compelling her marble-dark eyes and pointed chin and brown hair are. If I take her photo and show it to you, we will witness her beauty, and it's not that we'll be without compassion. It's that Sharbat's skin turned leathery, her daughter died, she had to walk three dangerous hours and drive another six from her remote Afghan village at the turn of the century to be reunited with the lauded photographer who took the heretofore only existent photograph of her, the one millions of people had seen that she herself hadn't.

It's that whatever Sharbat's green eyes demanded, in the photo we all consumed: we did not give to her.

*

I realize, slowly, what it will take. And I am afraid to tell you. I am afraid to ask this of myself.

I realize it when I ride in the early morning with Abu Faisal away from the airport in Turkey toward the Syrian border, and I am reminded by the nature of the sunlight and the geological landscape of Santa Maria, the closest city to my childhood home in California. And then when I am walking with the larger-than-life Dr. Mahrouz, the Syrian cardiologist who now lives in the U.K. and comes back monthly to deliver aid, on our first night all gathered in Reyhanli, in a high breeze on the main road in and out of town—it's after dinner, the breeze smells familiar, even the road is familiar, and we're headed back to the prosthetic limb center where we sleep and where a handsome young Syrian man who looks like my childhood friend Tristan and who lost his legs to Assad's shells is being rehabilitated— Dr. Mahrouz is telling me, by the roadside, after trotting to catch up with us because he stopped to investigate an opportunity to buy tomatoes and cucumber at a little stand. He's telling me of his time at school with Assad and the nature of Assad's megalomania: that Assad will raze his own people, crazed, until none of them exist before he surrenders because they are all *his*, the country is *his*, he is entitled to it and he won't stop—and I think of Highway 101, how this road is the Highway 101 of this place. And I will have to *make* it the 101. I will have to make it my family. My home. I will have to tell you—by which I mean tell myself, to understand it—that way. I am going to have to pick my favorite children in the world—Penelope and Max, who before I left San Francisco (I left out of Oakland and not Los Angeles in part so I could see them, before and after) piled on top of me in the hammock in the sun by their dad's garden in Oakland, who brought me raspberries cupped in their fingers, Penny with her impish eye gleam and Max with his face-creases in the morning, who draw with sidewalk chalk in matching tie-dye outfits and lay hands on my forearms as I read them stories—and you're going to have to pick yours.

And, in a place over and over again, a place only you can see that repeats like a mirrored tunnel: they're going to have to die.

III.

Imagine a ruin so strange it must never have happened.
—Barbara Kingsolver

The vineyards that surround my parents' ranch in Santa Barbara County, California, have been abandoned, and only dying grapevines remain. Rebels have taken up neighboring abandoned mansions as bases and used the wine cellars as stockpiling rooms and barracks. Government strongholds span the agricultural basin in central inland California where there used to grow a huge percentage of America's produce and where the California state water project is based, so most inland California irrigation has long since been switched off. The shortage is felt here and all throughout rebel-held territory, where canned goods were stored by sensible people branded as paranoid pessimists when the protests began. Those pessimists are now making a handy profit, though as the value of the US dollar descends into free-fall, they demand payment of other in-kind goods more and more often.

I drove upstate in one of my parents' old ranch vehicles, a dirty jeep covered in hay bits with AC vents smelling of mice, to bring Penelope and Max, down here on one of the last days the 101 was even vaguely passable, right before the opposition lost the Bay Area to government forces. Their parents, my cousin Cliff and his wife Dorothy, who let me watch them be adults and ask big life-questions as they hosted me every year over the last decade, were blown apart by a shell as Cliff dropped Dorothy off at the train station so she could attend a hearing in Sacramento as an environmental consultant. It was one of the first shells to fall in a days-long attack.

We were caught unawares; we thought government forces were going to attack Los Angeles first, and in any place that isn't under active attack, people attempt to conduct business as usual—as usual as possible. So they dropped off the kids, and drove to the train station, where Cliff died instantly in the explosion and Dorothy bled out slowly, trapped under a fallen pillar.

She knew, in her last moments, why no one helped her: by then we'd all heard that a second shell follows the first, to kill those who would run to aid the first victims.

It took some bribing and a few stretches of driving off-road both ways—Highway 101 was impassable in some places, littered with decaying body parts and exploded concrete and "checkpoints" of escaped prison convicts who claimed to be part of the rebel army—but I managed to get Max and Penelope back to the ranch, which had become our family's base of operations. My parents' siblings and all their children were in urban areas when the protests began. I found Penelope and Max late the night of their parents' death, finally asleep at a kind neighbor's house in Oakland. The rebels almost didn't let me into Oakland until I showed them pictures of the kids and begged. Across the water, in the heart of San Francisco, flames lit up the night sky. As their neighbor helped me load the car with Cliff and Dorothy's important documents, those contents of their dry pantry that hadn't been ransacked by desperate neighbors, and the kids' belongings, we could feel the explosions reverberate, shaking the flower vase on the windowsill.

The kids, exhausted from wailing, were somehow sound asleep, and I hoped that when they woke up, they would be on the ranch, and my mother would be there to talk them into the first steps they had to make: forward, into a strange life without their parents, in this strange place where all the plants were dying.

The protests began peacefully enough—Occupy demonstrations, the Ferguson demonstration, and the flagrant use of tear gas by police officers in riot gear at those demonstrations, prepared us for the reality that there would be protests in response to the Snowden leaks and that there would be local law enforcement crackdowns in response. But nothing prepared us for the news of the sheer extent of the NSA surveillance or the outpouring of demonstrators who took to the streets to voice their dissent. Twitter and Facebook enabled a coordinated protest in every major city in America with only a few hours of notice. It was an odd union of bedfellows; the Libertarians with their rifles wanting the government out of their house alongside Democrats who were appalled at the abuse of executive power.

First came news of gang rapes. In New Orleans, in Dallas, in the Bronx, in Los Angeles. There were bank robberies. There were black blocs of kids in San Francisco and Chicago with matching scarves wrapped around their mouths, readying themselves for tear gas and packing their backpacks with rocks they'd send into the windows of government offices, of Saks Fifth Avenue, and of large, pretty houses. There were lethal shoot-outs at fifty meters' distance between cops and civilians in St Louis, in Kansas City, in Las Vegas, in Orlando, in Minneapolis. Often gangs became the de facto lawmakers; in certain areas, they had been all along. Places like Compton, Baltimore, and Richmond, for this reason, held out the longest against the government, though its denizens were no less fearful than they'd been before. Gallows humor prevailed in the poorest areas, on reservations and in housing projects nationwide, as residents told one another with sad smiles that they had since birth already been in this, what looked to be a decades-long war.

Though the vineyards were dying out by the time they got here, Penelope and Max proved themselves awfully good at foraging the remaining grapes, because they grew up picking berries in their dad's garden. We tried for at least one of us to be watching them at first, but as things got worse we had to leave it to six-year-old Penelope to grow up enough to take care of her little brother without someone older there to kiss her elbow scrapes or soothe his cries. When there weren't angry young men patrolling our stretch of Foxen Canyon Road in packs, crowding into the backs of trucks and ransacking nearby wealthy actors' weekend homes and winemakers' villas, Penelope and Max would come out from a lean-to where they hid, looking for grapes. They called themselves rebels, those guys ransacking houses, so to the wider world we were part of their group—but they were still the kind of guys I taught Penelope and Max to hide from, holding their warm bodies close in the lean-to and putting a finger over my lips.

When they hid, they hid from some of our closest family friends from our pre-war life. My brother's best friend Len was big brother to my own best friend, Bea. The boys home-schooled together for a year when they were eleven and learned to build stanchions and milk goats in 4H. Our mother, who was seventy when the war broke out, learned alongside him and after the war began she kept the goat's grandkids alive, milked them daily, strained the cheese, scanned the skies for jets.

In the first days of the war, Bea and I didn't feel it much—it was not *our* houses, not *our* families. Then people started talking about genocide, the week before we were to shop for Bea's wedding dress. The day of our shopping date, I waited at our old carpool spot beside the 101 in the heat, texting and calling. No answer. Sometime that afternoon, a huge tank rumbled by. I jumped the white fence under the billboard on which a cowboy lassoed the words "Welcome to Los Olivos" and hid in the brush, hoping they wouldn't notice the dusty car in the shade. Thankfully the tank passed: they weren't going for Foxen Canyon—not today. But my stomach started to hurt as I realized that this meant Los Olivos was a no-go, and I understood that Bea, with whom I would chant "the mountains are following us!" on the way to school every day when we were small, could not be my friend anymore, and that although she was a mile away in Los Olivos I'd probably never see her again.

Once a schoolteacher, my mother had a big heart and allowed refugees from government-occupied areas to hide in the gulch littered with lupines in the spring, where my father roped a tire swing up for me from an oak branch in the 90s. We pleaded with her not to harbor refugees on the ranch, but she said she'd rather die in dignity than refuse good people a place to sleep. At dusk she would look up heavily from her garden, which was at the highest vantage point on the ranch, toward the string of lights that was Los Olivos, where our post office box was and where we couldn't go anymore. My mother's best friend Lydia, her colleague at the little country school that hadn't opened its doors in two years, also kept goats and had a garden in Los Olivos. Her son was forced into government service and his legs were blown off within a month. She looked after him, wheeled him around the house. She housed and fed some of her and our mother's old students— the ones caught on the government side—just as our mother did the ones caught on the rebels' side. We knew Lydia thought of our mother too, when she gardened and fed the former students they used to team-teach, when she handed them carrots and bags of milk before those former students, now teenagers with acne and braces, would strap guns to themselves and go out on missions from which they were unlikely to return.

Now that I think of it, we shouldn't have been surprised by the visit to the ranch from a government tank. Government forces of course knew that my cousin Cliff was in the Navy before becoming an engineer for a private company. They knew he had worked on submarines. Defectors who could have been of use to the government, and who had pledged explicit allegiance to the government before the war, were punished doubly. They weren't about to let Cliff's children survive. My mother tried to hide Penelope and Max in the pale yellow storage unit near the goat pasture where we stored my late grandmother's things. It didn't take the soldiers long to figure out where the children were crouching, in the mouse shit between big plastic tubs of memorabilia scribbled on with permanent marker.

In spite of the tank's size, my mother lunged in front of it and they cut her down so completely that I would later barely find a mangled limb to bury. The yellow-blistered bodies of Penelope and Max were paraded on top of the tank in Los Olivos that evening, evidence of what would happen to traitors, to government traitors, to their families. I wasn't there when they filled the storage unit with nerve gas, because other soldiers had discovered me hiding, huddled and shaken, behind the thick trunk of a sycamore in the creek bed, near the battered tents my mother had set up for neighbors trying to hide. I only glimpsed the yellow pallor of the children's skin from the clearing where the soldiers held me down as the tank rolled past, and I never heard them gagging or saw the muscle jerks spread to take the breath from them.

They left me to die, but one of the people hiding in the creek bed waited until nightfall and brought me to an old wine tasting room used as an elementary field hospital. I won't describe what the government soldiers did with me. I am a twenty-eight-year-old woman. I am a woman, period, and it happens to any woman here—to women cornered by "rebel" forces, also. The better kind of rebels were able, a week later—a week too late—to regain Foxen Canyon. It's been weeks since they brought me home, but I still struggle to sleep and struggle to get up, too, watching the flicks in my vision animate the ceiling of the barn loft, where they've put a cot for me. I try to remember when I would look at Penelope and Max and imagine having children, when I went home with cute UCSB students after dancing at a club all night because I liked having a body. Now all I do is hear the voice of my mother, humming the Fur Child song to Penelope and Max and their murmurs to her. Rebels walk outside, gravel crunching under their feet. I lie in my cot in the barn loft and watch a nimble daddy-long-legs spider craft a large web in the shadowy corner, where wood meets wood.

There was only one pair of eyes I was sure I didn't like. As we got near to the place in Atmeh camp where Karam Foundation built a playground—the fence around it had been robbed by residents of the camp by that time—a car approached. It's wasn't a very nice car. The guy in the car had bad eyes. They were empty. He spoke briefly with Abu Faisal from within the car. Abu Faisal stood with his thumbs linked through the straps of his backpack.

"What was that?" I asked as the car pulled away.

"Nothing," Abu Faisal said. "Nothing to worry about."

I asked again, and again he brushed me off. It's the only time he ever did so in the days we spent in Reyhanli and the day we spent in Syria, which is probably why it annoyed me so, and why I paid attention to it. At some point, Abu Faisal did explain a little more. The guy was doing his own patrol. He saw foreign people in the group, saw the chance to gain something. He patrolled not because anyone else wanted him to, but because he had decided it was his area. That, like the open sewage stream darkening the dust two feet outside the camp kitchen, where huge silver tureens housed one meal a day for the camp's residents, is perhaps what lack of infrastructure looks like: a river of shit and a pair of empty eyes.

I was at the border crossing between Syria and Turkey only weeks before the chemical attack in Damascus. That border crossing, Abu Faisal reports, is now closed for the most part. Over the weeks since we were there together, since we made that crossing and toured Atmeh refugee camp, it had become so dangerous that Turkey clamped down on the crossing points once controlled by the FSA. Humanitarian aid is even harder to deliver, now that the FSA is fighting Assad *and* extremist jihadists. The secular members of the FSA are the ones whose families were killed for protesting peacefully for a more democratic government. The jihadist factions are there because Assad is too liberal and modern for them. He is, in their eyes, not a ruthless dictator slaughtering his own people but an apostate, and *that's* why he needs to be done away with.

I was in Westgate mall in Nairobi, Kenya, typing up notes for this writing, in the week before Al-Shabaab terrorists responded to the presence of

Kenyan armed forces in Somalia by storming that mall and slaughtering innocent men, women, children, and babies. There was blood where I sat and typed, blood and screams everywhere, and the waitress with the very nicely groomed eyebrows whom I liked to talk with might be dead. Westgate's Israeli-owned cafe is the one the Al-Shabaab terrorists targeted. I would sit on its patio and order the grilled halloumi cheese salad, chatting with a waitress there about my work doing theater with Congolese refugee ladies in one of Nairobi's slums. I would put headphones in my ears and listen to the interviews I had recorded with Abu Faisal and Dr. Mahrouz, trying to type up Abu Faisal's hilarious summing-up of Thomas Friedman ("I think this! My moustache says this!") or Dr. Mahrouz talking shit about Assad's strange power plays with land and landmarks ("Fucking bitch," Mahrouz spouts off, "we don't need the lake.") remembering the cups of strong, brown tea we drank together.

At the border crossing near Atmeh, in Syria, had Assad's forces or jihadists attacked, as in the cafe in Westgate, my privilege would not have kept me alive; in fact, my blonde hair, blue eyes, pale skin, and lack of street smarts would probably have gotten me killed within the first minute. Instead, I flew to the United States on the 19th of September, two days before the carnage at the mall. The surest way to survive an event, after all, is not to attend it.

I spent a weekend in San Francisco with my cousins Cliff and Dorothy, and their children, who had not seized, defecated, suffocated, and foamed at the mouth until they were dead from nerve gas, but who had instead grown at least a half-inch each over the summer. I drove down the 101 in the sunshine, arriving at sunset at my new place, which I share with another new PhD, who was gone that evening.

I wandered the place alone, amazed that for the first time in over ten months I wouldn't be a guest, or at a hostel, or couch-surfing. I could see the stars. I could hear the crickets. I was less than an hour's drive from the ranch where I spent my childhood, where my parents brought me the day I was born. I woke up at sunrise and when I parted the curtains, there were two baby deer across the way under the oaks. As I drove from the mountains to campus on the beach, I remembered Syria; I remembered

Nairobi. I remembered the Charles Wright poem "Black Zodiac:" *What can we say to either of them? How can they be so dark and so clear at the same time?*

In my ears, Abu Faisal's letter, the one he sent after the 2013 chemical weapons attack outside of Damascus, rings like a bell: "The media and some world governments have even side-stepped the human loss of life all together, not even addressing it and jumped straight into 'The FSA bombed themselves with chemical weapons for world sympathy' story. The fact that supposedly educated people would even contemplate this, much less propagate this 'narrative'? If I debate this issue with 'them' then they already won. The massacre is forgotten and we've already gone academic."

Like the poet George Oppen, I cannot distinguish meaning from narrative. I think story is central to the human mind and the stories we hear and tell about the world are the way we make sense of it. I'm not sure how to give words on the response humans have to such horrors that did not happen to them. It did not happen to me: there is nothing to say about it.

I kept the nondescript messenger bag I'd brought into Syria at the gym in Nairobi, stuffed with the cheapest running shoes I could find after my old black ones floated away from me somewhere in an Istanbul hostel. I noticed their absence as I unpacked the big gray bag that Egypt Air lost for two days, the bag I had gone back to the Nairobi airport to fetch in the international terminal, the one that caught fire less than two days later, the terminal's blaze making world headlines.

There in the locker room, in September, in Nairobi, I'd put black duct tape on the shoes whose Velcro strips fell off in my hands the day after I bought them. I'd run on an elliptical. I'd ask to change the channel to CNN. I watched the Syria drama unfold because that's what it was: political theater. I accepted that words would always be part of that, that even my speech is that: a violent reduction of any uniqueness, usable to justify wars that aren't worth fighting and to avoid wars that are. It's malleable, and we can use it skate around difficult issues: we don't sugar-coat things with sugar. I turned twenty-nine on September 30th and it was the first day of my PhD seminar. Theories of Embodiment. We had to bring in a video or photo of something that would necessitate our giving undergraduate students a disclaimer.

I showed a YouTube clip two days old, a clip from Raqqa, where a school had been bombed. The disemboweled bodies loaded into a truck aren't recognizable as human. And yet, there is always the contingent of people who believe that this was, in fact, staged, as I explained to my graduate seminar. And we study performance, so let's pay attention to what convinces us. *We've already gone academic.* Let's talk about citizen journalism.

My birthday came and went; new friends swam with me in the Pacific; I got sand in my hair and my car. I jogged up the mountain roads and made it to the mouth of Rattlesnake Trial, sat on a rock with a top shaped like a dish that fit my body when I lay down and curled up in it, watching sideways as leaves fell in little gold bits down into the creek bed.

I drove my dented van to a compound off the grid in the Los Padres mountain range where a Chumash native named Tautahcho lived with his family in houses they built. Tautahcho, or "T," has known me over half my life, since before I ever left America, since before I ever had sex or participated in a protest.

I bring T carved owls from each country I work in. They live in nooks in his earthen house. I am technically agnostic, but I do believe that I've survived my sometimes-dicey experiences abroad because T sends a pack of guardians to watch over me, bouncer spirits with the brawn of Mr. Clean. There on December 21st, T led the Winter Solstice ceremony at his home on the mountain, informing the twelve of us gathered there that his work was difficult, but that he was the only one left around here who knew how to do it: how to open the West Gate to the valley of the shadow, where the spirits of the dead live. He warned us that the spirits of the dead would heed our prayers but especially because we were speaking in English we needed to be very specific. "Don't just ask for every person on earth to have water," he told us, "because you might end up with a monsoon. And sometimes the spirits can be frightening when they visit, so be prepared for that."

Over the course of the first five hours of the circle (which were all I stayed awake for), after we all stood and threw tobacco into the flames, the fire burned and people drummed and we could come and go from the circle at will. Inside the cook shack, we feasted. I asked T whether I could bring my journal by the fire and write what I had to say to the spirits. I was thinking of what I wished for the children at Atmeh, specifically, the girl with the dark eyes whose picture I had decided not to take. I didn't want to get it wrong.

In response, T held up a mason jar and looked at me through it, so he blurred.

"That would be like this," he said. "Why make it harder for the spirits to hear you?" That night, my phone downloaded a message from Abu Faisal: Dr. Mahrouz, the larger-than-life cardiologist who was always absconding from little gardens with vegetables for us to eat during our days in Reyhanli, whose booming voice made lewd jokes and who, along with his brothers, was a de facto leader of the village of Maarrat al-Nu'man, had been kidnapped by ISIS eight days prior.

He had not wanted to give in to them because if he did, the civilians of Maarrat would be subject to the law of ISIS, one of the Al-Quaeda affiliate "rebel" groups. Over the next two years ISIS would grow stronger and more fundamentalist by the day, the world watching in horror as members beheaded Japanese journalists and American aid workers alike.

I had no context for what might be happening to Dr. Mahrouz at that moment—were they torturing him? Was he cold? Did he have shelter?— and thought mainly of his fifteen-year-old daughter, one of his three girls, who was so recognizably teenage in her beauty and awkwardness, who had come with us into Atmeh, and who probably was much less young after this week. He was meeting with ISIS to suss out some conflicts between them and the civilians of Maarrat, and when things got heated, the ISIS bodyguards took him. Dr. Mahrouz is stubborn, with expansive hospitality and expansive humor and a belly laugh, and he chose not to give in to the "rebels" whom the media knows as the now de facto face of the opposition. I crept to T's stepdaughter's house, and slept in one of the little nooks in the corner, somehow unable to bring these ghosts to the fire. Dr. Mahrouz's booming voice. The warm sun shining through the leaves of vegetables in his hands. His jokes about Angelina Jolie.

I slept until the blue of dawn, falling to sleep in a jumble of images of the doctor and the night before Solstice, when one young man, another "child" of T's who lives on the mountain with his wife and two sons, made a fire as part of his monthly fasting ritual on the patio.

A few of us joined him, warming our hands and feet as the stars appeared beyond the oak branches. The young father's youngest, who is two, clambered onto his dad's lap as we talked and Bamboo, the kitty with a dog's personality, puddled into purrs in the boy's lap, so they were a father-son-kitty pile melting together by the fire. I looked at the clear night sky, and at the boy sandwiched between a purring cat and his father bending over him, and I thought this is what every child deserves and so few of them get.

And so I was already thinking of them, of the children who followed us around in the dry heat at Atmeh, with dirty skin and fathomless eyes, with candy bars to sell us or empty bottles to jump on and frighten us with the gunshot noise that only we weren't used to, when the young father asked: *what's the most intense experience you've ever had?*

What is intensity in human life, and how is it measured? When does an experience begin and end? I could say, the day I went in for an IUD insertion at Planned Parenthood around my 25th birthday and they couldn't put it in because the morning-after pill hadn't worked and I was twelve days pregnant, the feeling I had then, or the poem I wrote to the unborn child I wasn't ready for, whose mother wouldn't have a house, a viable income, or a spouse. But where does that experience begin and end? Sex is an intense thing, and it's what caused the fertilization, so would that experience begin there, and end with the writhing on a gurney and a mound of blood tissue in a Dixie cup?

Or would it end with the work I began in 2011 with refugee women from Congo in Nairobi, and how I believe the spirit of the person I asked to wait and come back again when I was better able to provide for children is what guided me and made me able to do that work, work with girls who don't have mothers of their own anymore and whom I wouldn't have traveled to Africa to meet if I'd had a ten-month-old? Where does the most intense experience of my life begin and end?

I went to Atmeh camp just inside Syria on the three-year anniversary of my due date. I went into Atmeh and looked into the eyes of these children, all of whom may now be dead of explosives or hunger or cold, on the due date of the baby I didn't bear. Does the experience end there? Does it end in the marble-dark eyes of the most beautiful girl I have ever seen, who reminded me of the photograph of Sharbat?

At the fire I didn't speak of my own child. I spoke of the ones who already came into the world, and who might already be dead. I said that the knowledge that I would leave and continue living a comfortable, rewarding life and that these children could not leave that place among the olive trees engendered a feeling I don't think there are words for.

The next morning in the blue of dawn I awakened and walked to the cook shack, where T sat with some coffee. He had charcoal smeared on his face, and explained to me: "At first light, just now, I performed the ceremony that closes the gate once again, the one to the west, and I had to disguise myself, so I'm not taken."

My professor explained a few things about Descartes and Ponty to me when I came to his office hours: phenomenology's attention to the process of getting to the point when we realize we're in a body, when we realize that we're thinking. After leaving his office I put on my duct-taped shoes, I aimed for a run around the lagoon right by the theater building, and got about fifty meters, and then the ocean was there. The shoes came off. I went in, slowly, level by level of cold banding my body. The breakers were a little relentless, but beyond them there was calm—suddenly deep water, the dark suggestions of kelp.

The mountains beyond campus, which I could see from my spot in the water, were striped with vegetation. When we were little, a friend called them ice-cream mountains because the plant matter looked like chocolate syrup on the mountains from far away. I paddled, I did what I do when I try to meditate, and felt the swaying to and fro of my body being carried along by the sea. The sun hammered down, chinking the water with points of bright. I recited my name and the date to myself, wiggled my fingers and toes. The swaying was easy.

What was it like before you realized you were you? My professor had asked.

I remember the first moment I thought, 'I'm me,' I had answered.

And before that?

Nothing. I didn't know I was like other people. That inside of the people I saw were consciousnesses like mine: that I was in something that looked a lot

43

like them. I didn't know I looked like a person. Being inside my own body was so different from looking at someone else's.

Easy, sway, kelp, calm.

Värmland County, Sweden

WHAT YOU WAIT FOR

CHAPTER I

There is a certain look in the eye: shadows beneath. The bare apartment. The premature worry lines about the face. The sun on a quiet kitchen table where there sits a stack of language worksheets, meticulously completed in pencil on graph paper. Headphones in a knot, Arabian sweet rolls covered in sesame seeds next to the green Q'uran which he says you can touch: the book but not the words within—"unless you"—he makes a motion with his hands—"washing," you say, and he nods, rubbing his chest—he rubs his chest often, over the course of the time you spend together. It hurts sometimes. His chest.

On the windowsill of the bedroom are the only objects in it besides the narrow twin bed itself: a plant, a Santa and Mrs. Claus figurine, a panda bear, and a teddy bear. He will give you the clothes off his back. He will give you his soul, he tells you, but he couldn't part with these four objects.

He shows you a picture of his fiancée on Facebook: an undeniably attractive young woman, posing knowingly, an arm behind her jet black hair, arresting the camera with ice blue eyes. He calls her his panda. He thinks she is like a panda, so when he saw a panda in a store here in a tiny Swedish village, he bought it. When he misses her, he holds it, strokes it, talks to it. The teddy bear and the plant, she sent to him from Syria. The Santa and Mrs. Claus porcelain figurine he bought during the holidays. He's a Muslim, but he respects Christmas, respects that the Swedes he lives among find it a meaningful holiday, so he wanted to buy something. He was on a chat app with his fiance and saw from the sidewalk this figurine in a local shop. He showed her the figurine through real-time video. "Buy it!" she prompted him. "It's us."

It's not an easy road. He's a passionate man, and she's a passionate woman. They fight. They might end it. He filed the paperwork for her to join him, but he needs to be resettled in Sweden for eighteen months first. They came together six months before he left Syria, six months before the third time he was imprisoned in one of Assad's jails, and the friend who bailed him out warned him: "Leave. Leave now. If you value your life, your mother, your woman. Get out, or you'll be killed."

So he did, and he will, over the coming hours, tell you a story of his odyssey: months of pain, the insides of three different countries' jails. Now, in July, Santa and Mrs. Claus hold one another, cheerful red and green, and the Swedish summer afternoon is so warm he has opened the door to his balcony. The balcony where he can stand for hours, and no one will greet him. No one will come out to their balcony across the way. No one will wave, or ask how he is. There is no neighborhood. Just a handful of apartment blocks near the only market. Two restaurants, one in the train station. In one of two pots he owns, he makes coffee for you, after first insisting that Arabian coffee won't be good for you and running out to buy 7-up and Swedish coffee with milk in it. After a few hours he stubs out his fourteenth cigarette into one of his small tea saucers and stands, spooning the grounds into the pot of warm water, telling you that when he closes his eyes and inhales, he is home. "My homeland is in this cup," he says, returning to the table. "My mother, when she makes it."

He's thirty-four. He was a lawyer in Aleppo. His Swedish teachers, who are some of the only people consistently kind to him, tell him his future is bright and he'll shine in whatever he does in his new life here. He can show you Youtube videos of the impassioned speeches he gave as the leader of his group of lawyers. "Every Syrian child is my child!" he yells in Arabic. "All Syrians are my family. Assad must go. He can't tear us apart."

He was in a fight with his brother, he tells you, but not the nature of the disagreement, or if the brother is the one out of his seven biological siblings who was resettled to Sweden also. After all, you're his family now, too; he told you in a Whatsapp text before even meeting you in person that "you are my syster from this moment."

You understood what that meant. You understood that, like every Syrian man you have met, his mother probably told him to help anyone who asks and to do anything for a guest. You understand that he would have slept on the floor and insisted you take the small sofa, since the little twin bed wasn't even there when you arrived yesterday from Karlstad. His Dutch friend Lucas, who gave you both the ride, needed to go home to his wife and two small girls after spending all day helping Ahmad vacate wherever he had been staying to this new apartment. The car was packed with four pieces of luggage that Ahmad had brought on four buses before Lucas picked him up and the two drove to the nearest train station in Karlstad to collect you.

"He always tried to kiss my daughter on the lips," said Lucas in a low voice as Ahmad unloaded his bags. "If I were you, I wouldn't stay here. I think he's a good guy, but I've only known him for two months, and there is nothing in that apartment. There's nowhere for you to sleep. He just has one couch. Not even a bed."

You wished you'd had longer than a half hour in the backseat of the car, trying to hear Ahmad's quiet, exhausted voice over the engine as the car flew through placid, emerald-grassed fields, to gauge his character. You were in Sweden on the way back from a conference, staying with a friend of the family in Stockholm for a few days. You'd read that in July 2013, Sweden became the first nation in the European Union to offer permanent residency to any Syrian who made it there. So you wrote Abu Faisal, the Syrian-American who brought you into Syria to tour a refugee camp in 2013, asking if there were any Syrian refugees in Sweden he knew of whom you might meet. Abu Faisal connected you and Ahmad on Whatsapp a few days ago. Ahmad is somewhere in Abu Faisal's extended network of family and friends, and Abu Faisal hasn't met him but knows from mutual friends that he's a standup guy. The cobweb of relations that makes up the Syrian diaspora has never failed to protect you with its implicit family-checks and balances, and you didn't want to assume the worst about the man leaning on his knees in the doorway. Ahmad's story, you knew, had to be a harrowing one. Making it to Sweden from Syria is an odyssey by any mode of travel, for anyone, let alone for an unwanted refugee fleeing for his life from the worst conflict this century has known.

You accompanied Lucas to the door of the apartment building, where Ahmad stood on the doorjamb, panting next to the pile of bags he's just schlepped from the car.

"Would you like help bringing these up the steps?" you asked, gesturing to the bag.

He shook his head, hand on his chest.

"Okay," said Lucas, "we will go then. She'll come to you tomorrow by bus."

"You can stay here," said Ahmad to you, his forehead creasing.

"That's okay," you said. "There's a youth hostel nearby. I'll come back tomorrow when we are both less sleepy. You're tired and I woke up with a cold. Tomorrow, after you have rested, we can have the whole day to talk."

Your heart was a little heavy as you took in his disappointed look. You'd only met him an hour ago, he had one sofa for you both to sleep on, you were a young single woman, and he was clearly lonely—perhaps desperate, you couldn't tell—and you didn't want to be stupid. But if your fears were unfounded, it was not a good thing, to turn down what Abu Faisal once called "legendary Arab hospitality." You felt you were denying Ahmad the chance to claim that one piece of his history back, to express one of the best things about the culture that had given him himself, along with all the other pieces that time, distance, and trauma had ripped away: Ahmad was raised to sleep on the floor for you.

"Okay," he said softly.

You waved. He waved. As you and Lucas left, two pale adolescent guys, one of whom is on rollerblades,—"*helping* in quotation marks," Lucas chuckles—carry a small twin bed along the outside of the deserted roundabout nearby. It's only the next day, when you see that little bed there in the bedroom, near his teddy bear and his panda, his Christmas figurine, that you understand unequivocally that the little bed had been meant for you.

CHAPTER II

Before the revolution, Ahmad lived a quiet life in Aleppo's Al Sakhour neighborhood. There was a blind cigarette seller named Saeed there whom Ahmad liked quite a lot; even though he was blind, Saeed always gave back exact change. Ahmad only bought cigarettes from Saeed, despite the fact that nearby shops sold the same brand he smoked.

On a Friday—the usual day for protests at the start of the revolution—Saeed was standing on his usual corner when a protest started nearby at a mosque. Ahmad was also nearby, but did not join in the demonstration, which was quickly broken up by Assad regime thugs shooting at the crowd. Three people were killed, including Saeed, who was not even a part of the protest.

Muslims are buried the same day they die, before sunset. At the funeral that night, Ahmad was so distraught for Saeed that he actually went to prepare Saeed's body for burial with others, to wash the body and wrap it in a white cloth. At the funeral-march to the graveyard, Ahmad got onto someone's shoulders and chanted slogans against the regime for the first time in his life.

*

Two weeks later, Ahmad joined a small protest by the lawyers' union in Aleppo against the regime, and he filmed it with his phone. He gave the film to a friend during the protest, and it was broadcasted on Al Jazeera next day. He was arrested at the demonstration and had to promise never to protest the regime again before he was released. But he did, and he became the protest leader in Aleppo for the lawyers' union. Twice at various protests, hired regime thugs tried to stab him.

A few months after the FSA took over half of Aleppo (including his neighborhood), Ahmad joined the Free Lawyers' Union in Aleppo and organized new laws and rules for the "liberated" half of Aleppo. The union base was attacked multiple times by regime planes; they disbanded soon after. He started organizing aid and well-being campaigns in his neighborhood, but was abducted by the regime again. Luckily, a high-ranking "neutral" lawyer who knew Ahmad got him out of the regime prison. He kept up his activism, despite receiving threats from various militias, until a friend on the regime side of Aleppo soon told him to leave, because the regime was going to kill or arrest him soon.

That was 2013.

Ahmad left for Turkey. He first went to Gaziantep, where he looked for work for a month, but found none because he didn't speak Turkish. He went then to Istanbul, which was even more expensive than Gaziantep, bigger. "You have to pay even for water there," Ahmad says. "Not like in the Arab world."

Ahmad found a tall, large, very dark-skinned Syrian man named Musab. Syrians went to him for passage to Greece. Musab was very tall and fat and always asked his refugee customers for things if he knew they were coming from Syria. Musab always told everyone he'd pay them back when he met them but he never did.

Abu Faisal writes: "You would give Musab the coffee and cigarettes he asked for and pretend you didn't want the money (as is kind of a custom in our culture if someone asks you for something) and then he would never offer to pay (which, in our culture, he's then supposed to say 'Oh no, please, here is the money'). Musab would ask every single refugee to bring him the same things, and it looked like he had a huge side business taking the cigarettes and coffee from people to sell on the black market. He asked everyone to always bring two cartons of cigarettes and one kilogram of coffee. (Side note: Syrian cigarettes are popular in Turkey because they are cheap compared to Turkish market cigarettes.) Before the revolution most of these people-smugglers were cigarette-smugglers, I'm not sure if I showed this to you on our trip in Reyhanli, but in the hills next to where we slept, on the Syrian side of the border, you can see faint headlights way up high in the mountains. Those are trucks belonging to the smugglers using the same routes before the revolution to smuggle, only the 'product' has changed from cigarettes to people."

Greece is often the destination from Turkey for Syrians, because from Greece, one can possibly reach many other parts of the world. Germany, France, Italy, Denmark, the Netherlands. He agreed to pay Musab 1,200 euro for passage in an inflatable boat from Izmir, Turkey, to the Greek island of Lesbos, and its city of Mytilene.

Ahmad shows me a picture on his cell phone. "Name *balam*," he says. It looks to me more like a raft, impossibly small, more like the kind used by vacationing jet skiers on lakes in Michigan. They were to take the *balam* for two and a half hours, from Izmir to Mytilene. Somehow twenty people were supposed to fit in it.

Ahmad stayed in Musab's Istanbul apartment for five days with sixteen other people hoping for passage to Greece. On the sixth day they piled into a van in Istanbul, a Turk admonishing them to keep silent and beating them when they didn't. "We feel"—Ahmed mimics suffocating, sitting on his kitchen floor beside my chair, wrapping his arms around his chest—"for twelve hours."

After the twelve-hour ride from Istanbul, they arrived at Izmir at 3 a.m. The *balam* was meant for twenty people; there were thirty-five passengers. It was dark and cold, and they didn't know what would happen.

"Who will drive the boat?" they asked.

"One of you," the burly Turk answered.

"But none of us know how."

"Sure you do. Choose anyone from the group to do it. It's easy. Just take the wheel."

Someone volunteered, and the thirty-five refugees crammed into the boat. After two hours in the cold night at sea, they got five kilometers away from Mytilene. And there it was: a Greek coast guard ship.

"Stop," said the police over loudspeaker to the refugees, who were crowded there below on the water, shifting on the waves, squinting in the bright lights of the large, imposing ship. "Don't come. Go back."

"Help," they answered. "We have children. We need help. We don't feel safe in our country. We are Syrian."

"Go back," the police answered again. This time they fired shots in the air. The children were terrified.

The thirty-five refugees huddled on the boat for a few minutes while the Greek officers conferred above. Finally the officer turned to them and said, "Okay."

"Okay?"

"You're our friends. We'll help you. We'll bring you onto our boat."

The refugees were more relieved than Ahmad can express. The Greek coast guard took the raft and helped the refugees board the ship, towing the orange boat behind them for a kilometer or so.

But the Greek coast guard didn't take them to Mytilene. They took them to Turkish waters, forced them back onto their little inflatable boat, only without the motor. And they left them there, singing "Bye bye!" as they motored off.

"Bye bye," half-sings Ahmad, waving his hand, pain twisting his face. "Like Mr. Bean. Can you imagine?"

*

After half an hour, packed and shivering on that motorless inflatable boat in the dark, someone finally called the Turkish police.

"Help us. We're in the middle of the sea. We have no motor. We're going to die. We have women and children."

A half hour later, a Turkish police ship appeared. Officers in orange shirts brought out their cameras first, insisting on filming the refugees answering "Syria" to their questions before allowing them on the ship and corralling them onto the land.

Morning. After six hours of waiting in the sun, the police brought a sandwich and tea for each Syrian. They were allowed to smoke, but not to leave. "We're your friends," said the Turkish police. "If anyone is sick, we'll bring them directly to the hospital."

The rest were brought to the police station in a bus around noon. They took the Syrians' fingerprints, baggage, and money. They had to stay the night in jail while the Turkish police ran background checks.

They all got showers, beds, blankets, and food. They were allowed to smoke and use their phones. They were released the next day with their money and baggage.

Ahmad called Musab, the honcho to whom he'd paid 1,200 euros for passage to Greece.

"I'm not in jail anymore," an exhausted Ahmad mumbled into the receiver. "I don't know what to do."

"Don't worry," came the answer. "It was bad luck. You almost got to Greece. Come to Istanbul now."

"But Musab, I'm too tired to come all the way back to Istanbul. It's been so hard. It'll take another twelve hours to go all the way back."

"So? You still need to come. My rules."

So Ahmad spent the money for another long bus trip to Istanbul. It caused him pain. He called his mother.

"Please," she begged him, "Come back. Do it for me. I'm afraid you won't survive this. You'll be eaten by sharks. You're about to get married. Come for me and for your bride."

"No, Mom. The Syrian regime will catch me. There's nothing for me in Syria. I have to go to Europe. I'll be safe there and I can find a job. I can live a good life with my wife."

The story begins to play out like a high-stakes but slow-paced Groundhog Day. The same van with the windows you can't see into in Istanbul's Taksim square. The same driver, the same Turk who beats the passengers into twelve hours of cramped, claustrophobic silence. At 9 p.m., they arrived in Izmir once again. There were even more than thirty-five people in this group for the inflatable boat. When Ahmad saw the *balam*, then the amount of people, including a Somali woman three times his size, his heart sank.

Ahmad is quick to clarify that he is not afraid of death. If he stayed in Syria, he'd die. "I have no problem," he says simply. "I have nothing to lose. If I stay in Syria, maybe I'll be sitting in my apartment and a bomb will drop on it. When I die, I die. This is from G-d. Maybe after you go now, today," he tells me, "I die. We don't know."

After one kilometer the boat collapsed.

Everyone needed to swim the kilometer back to shore or die.

Eventually, they all made it to shore. They hid on the beach, soaking, crouching behind bushes so as not to be seen by the police. After two hours, three cars appeared. Musab's cars. They took the refugees in groups of six. They were lodged in a hotel in the Basmane area of Izmir—ironically, a hotel near the police station. It was early in the morning, yet again. Ahmad was beyond exhausted, and felt insane, furious: "like I'm going to break everything around me. I need to go. I think Musab's a liar."

If you traffic desperate people who need to get out of one place and into another, Ahmad has learned, you must be a bad person, a person who doesn't respect the lives and souls of others, who sees those others as sheep, as animals, as nothing. They just want your money. Ahmad shakes his head. "No honest one works with this job," he says.

So, the next day Ahmad decided to stop working with Musab. He stayed for two weeks in Izmir. He went to a cafe in Basmane near the police station, where, speaking what he calls "the eyes language," a person looking for passage elsewhere can find ten or fifteen people willing to do it for a price. There he found someone, an Egyptian called Ali, who said he could get Ahmad out. A twenty-minute ride on a ship, for 1,500 euro.

"You have to check out of the hotel you're in," Ali ordered him. "Stay in this other hotel and call when you're ready."

"But I don't have the money for that hotel and the passage too."

"That's how I do it. Those are my rules. If you can't respect them, then piss off. I can find another one just like you, someone who'll do things my way without any trouble. So when I call you, be ready."

After two days at the expensive hotel Ali suddenly needed another 200 euro, so now it was 1700. Ahmad's heart sank further. He went back to the cafe, tried to find someone who wasn't such a scam artist. A Somali. A Sudanese guy. Finally, desperate, humbled, he called Musab.

"Hello. Musab. Can you help me?"

"No. You went to someone else. I'm not going to help you again."

"Please, Musab. I'm alone. I have no money. You're Syrian, you understand. Please. Help me."

"Fine. Wait for my call."

Two hours later, Musab called with the order to come back to Istanbul yet again.

"But I'm already here," argued Ahmad, as he had before. "Why go back twelve hours and then ride in the van to Izmir again? It's twenty-four hours and twenty Turkish lira."

"You want to work with me again, you do as I say."

So Ahmad paid again, and rode again, and arrived in Istanbul in the morning. Three hours later, he went right back to Izmir with the same van, same driver, the same conditions. For all twelve hours from Istanbul to Izmir, the driver was on the phone, narrating in Turkish every single move he made. Ahmad didn't know much Turkish, but he gathered that the driver was learning of possible police blocks and driving around them, sometimes pulling over to wait, admonishing the passengers in an alarmed whisper to shut up.

"This time is twenty-five people," says Ahmad with a grin. "I was surprised. Twenty-five is a good number. And everyone is thin! It's good."

Ahmad's heart told him he'd arrive this time. In the boat he was so bone-tired that he actually slept for half an hour. He saw in his dream the sun, and a clock on the wall that said six o'clock, and a baby laughing at him. When they finally arrived in Greece, his dream came true. They arrived at six, and on the beach he saw a woman, holding a laughing baby in the sun.

CHAPTER III

On that third perilous attempt at crossing to Greece from Turkey by water in an inflatable raft, Ahmad woke up after a half hour of sleep. He'd dreamt of a baby smiling in the sun, and a clock that said six. The first thing he did was look at his watch, which said six o'clock. And the first people he saw on the beach—the beach at Myteline on the island of Lesbos—was a woman and a laughing baby.

"My dream come true!" he tells me in his quiet Karlstad apartment, the Swedish summer green and warm outside. He waves his fifth cigarette around. "My dream!" he says again.

The refugee who drove the boat did not need to pay Musab, the human trafficking "gangster" Ahmad worked with, then didn't work with, then begged to take him back as his hope ran out in Turkey. It was Musab's way or the highway, so to speak, and Musab had given knives to four of the passengers. He instructed those passengers, three who were from Pakistan and one who was from Afghanistan, to puncture the boat once it landed successfully at Myteline. The Greek police, they were told, would put them back on the boat if the boat was functional, instead of bringing them to the police quarters at Myteline.

Two strong policemen appeared, demanding to know of the beleaguered group how much they had paid for the journey, and who the gang leader was. Musab was not the gang leader; he was a henchman who paid the Turkish guy above him, and so on. Ahmad and his fellow passengers had no idea who Musab answered to.

Everyone was interrogated. They turned to Ahmad. "Well?" one asked. "Who drove the boat?"

"I don't know," said Ahmad. "I was asleep. I was tired. I'm not sure. I don't know."

But one of the other Syrians pointed to the guy who'd driven the boat: "It was him."

The man who'd driven the boat was taken away in handcuffs.

"And who punctured the boat? Tell us."

Again, a few of the Syrian passengers lifted their hands to point at the Pakistanis and the Afghani. The driver got ten years in jail, and those who punctured the boat got six.

"The Greek laws are strong," Ahmad says simply.

Ahmad's group stayed on the beach for two days. People from Human Rights Watch came. Ahmad recites the memory: "'Hello. How are you? What's your name? Where are you from? What do you need? Do you prefer pasta or rice? Hamburger? What do you need? We are here for you. We can help you. We respect you. We will bring food for you. Don't be afraid. Feel safe, you are in Europa.' 'I need jacket,' 'Ok I will bring,' 'I need food', 'Ok I will bring', 'I need sim card', 'Ok I will bring you', 'I need cover', 'Ok I will'" —Ahmad interrupts himself—"they were so—they were so *kind*."

After the third day on the beach at Myteline, Ahmad and his twenty-or-so traveling companions got a certain paper from the Greek government via the police station. "Arabian name *kharziya*," Ahmad tells me. "*Kharziya* is: welcome to Greece. You come to Greece with illegal way. You must to go out six months from this date. Paper with your picture here. You come illegal way but after this you are legal. After you have *kharziya*, they say you are free."

They took his fingerprint and his picture, checked his eyes and his lungs. They told him that a big ship would take him from Myteline to Athens.

When I ask about the sort of boat, he calls his friend to send him a picture. He's annoyed when the friend doesn't pick up. "I hate it when they don't answer," he says. "When people call me, I answer."

He looks up at me from his phone. "You drink Seven?" he asks. "Arabian coffee?"

"I'll try some," I say. I am smiling because Ahmad would not hear of my drinking Arabian coffee earlier this afternoon. He was convinced I wouldn't enjoy it.

"I have nothing to make coffee," he says above the din of the water rushing from the faucet into one of his two pans.

"I'm not worried," I say in a sing-song voice. He sings back.

"This is for yooooou," he sings, "and this is for meeee."

I laugh.

"I feel good when I'm talking to other people," he says suddenly.

I imagine a warm, dry place full of family where he was at home. I try to picture a bustling Aleppo, packed with his countrymen, the daily prayers on loudspeakers, the smells of the foods he grew up eating wafting down the streets outside his law school.

"I think humans are meant to be in community," I say. "It makes us sick when we are alone."

Over the following months, as we keep in touch on Whatsapp, it becomes clear that Ahmad's feelings about being in Sweden are as complex and volatile as his feelings about Ranim, who he loves in the sort of push-me-pull-you way that two young people do who have passion for one another. They were in love for six months before he had to leave Syria. He is grateful to be in Sweden, but thinks sometimes that it would have been better to stay in Syria, especially when his brother-in-law dies in February 2016 from a Russian bomb. What keeps him going into 2016 is Ranim's imminent arrival, approved in the winter by the Swedish government. Ranim, who he says is like a panda.

There in Ahmad's bare apartment in summer 2015, as he makes coffee, I think again about the noise, greeting kisses, and physical touch I have observed between people from Arabian backgrounds. I think about the reserved nature of the Swedes I've spoken with this week. It must be lonely for him. Lonely to his very bones. Who will he make coffee for? Who will he sing to?

Of the refugee experience in Sweden, Ahmad says, pouring the coffee, "We have nothing… to, to, to *do*. We don't have to make decision. We just come. But we don't know where we go, and what to do. Just come to the safe place."

"Right," I say, tasting the coffee and lighting another cigarette.

"People like you think," he continues. "Not kind, very kind. It's normal. Some people kind and some people no, like any people in the world. Like America, there is kind and there is no kind." I nod. He continues: "I have experience with everyone from Izmir, to Mytelini, to Istanbul to Athens, I have a lot, I can speak until you end this"—he gestures to my phone, which is recording—"I don't know if you can hear everything I can say, whether I can continue—"

"Tell the story!" I say. "You finally arrived in Athens."

"Ah," he says, in a way I can't decode.

"What's going on?" I say.

"How you like drink coffee?" he asks.

"Like you do," I say.

"Like what?"

I laugh, and start singing the *"smoking cigarettes and watching captain kangaroo / no, don't tell me I've nothing to do"* song from the *Pulp Fiction* soundtrack. I'm pumped full of Robitussin to try and be less cold-and-flu-ish for these precious few hours with Ahmad, but perhaps it's caught up with me. Ahmad is also loosey-goosey, perhaps just from having a guest after long days alone. He sing-song-speaks as he fixes our coffee. He rummages in his fridge and holds up a package.

"We eat this for Ramadan," he says.

"Isn't Ramadam over?" I say.

"Every day is like Ramadan," he grins.

We meander back to his odyssey.

"Where we?" his forehead crinkles.

"Athens," I say.

He lights another cigarette.

Ahmad was exhausted after finally receiving his *kharziya,* but the first thing he did was call his mother: "I've arrived, Mom. I'm well, I promise. I'll keep going. I won't forget you, and I'll try to bring you to live with me." Then he calls his fiancée, Ranim, to tell her the same thing.

The ship to Athens, he recalls, was wonderful. It was huge, and filled with people from Ireland, from Turkey, from Sweden. He bought the economy ticket for sixty-five euros, and slept between seats for a whole seven hours. When they arrived in Athens at 7 a.m., Ahmad couldn't believe he was in Europe. It was like an Arabian country. He saw people from Pakistan, Afghanistan, Iraq, Egypt, and Syria; he saw Arabian cafes, Arabian supermarkets, and even more Arabian people; he saw people from Bulgaria and Serbia begging for money.

He set off immediately for his father's brother, who lived near Acharnon Street and owned an Arabian cafe there. He lived there with his uncle until he could find another guy like Musab, this time to take him to the Netherlands, which Ahmad calls his "dreamland".

"Why the Netherlands?" I ask.

"Because they have a"—he looks up the word in English on his phone—"church." They have a church. To help you to study for free. They don't look on your religion. It doesn't matter. They respect human. Any religion. Any nationality. We respect human people who thinks like that. We respect Christian people. So before Finland, and they say Netherlands has good—not like here, always winter."

"Good weather," I say. My imagination wanders again to the desert sun, to the noises and smells written in his mind.

Ahmad was also partial to the idea of France. He thought about France. In particular, he thought about the Eiffel Tower. But in order to get to any of those places—to France, to the Netherlands, to Finland—he had to find a new Musab.

CHAPTER IV

Once he had rested up at his uncle's place in Athens, Ahmad resumed his search for another human trafficker to help him get from Athens to a safe place further north.

He found Ali, a guy who was, like Musab, Egyptian. "You look Czech!" Ali told Ahmad. Ahmad didn't believe him. He thought he could pass for Italian, sure; for Spanish, maybe; for Bulgarian, okay; but not Czech or Danish or Swedish or anything. They have another kind of skin, another kind of hair, another kind of everything, but here Ali was telling him he'd be able to go to the airport in Athens, say hello, get in his seat, and congratulations, bye bye! For five thousand euros, Ali was sure, Ahmad could waltz into a Greek airport and board a plane for a safer place.

The money Ahmad paid Ali wasn't his. It came from his uncle, who saved from owning a restaurant; from his fiancée, who sold her jewelry, from others.

The way Ahmad found Ali was standard: he went to a certain cafe where those sorts of people hung out, waiting to be approached by refugees in need of a way out, by people called "migrants" or "drifters" or "ne'er-do-wells." "Don't worry," they'd say. "I'm a professional. I've helped a thousand people before you."

"Like a king," says Ahmad wryly. "Like an emperor. 'Don't worry, don't be afraid.'"

These people, from Ahmad's perspective, had no problems. No stress. They had money, cars, homes. They felt good, while the people who needed them felt bad. Ahmad felt frozen: he couldn't spend one euro without worrying about how he'd pay it back. He'd often go without food. He knew that he just needed to get to the safe place—Sweden, or Denmark, or Iceland, the Netherlands, some place else—and then he'd be able to receive some kind of assistance. His life might have in it a television, some food, maybe a fridge, a table, a place to go to school.

The usual escrow-style agreement was reached with Ali: an office protected Ahmad's 5,000 euros under his password until Ahmad arrived safely at his destination, at which point Ali would receive it. Ahmad's first leg (of this part of his odyssey, anyway) took the form of a big ship from Athens to Crete, a journey that lasted for thirteen hours and cost him forty-five euro. He remembers that the hotel in Crete was a good hotel. He waited for Ali to call, and when he did, he told Ahmad he'd be leaving the next day with a Czech passport. Ali's people gave Ahmad the passport, but wouldn't go near the airport. Getting caught, for them, meant twenty years in prison.

Ahmad still wondered at their fear. They had so much money, and lived like kings in Athens with lots of women and nice cars.

At the airport Ahmad made it past the first metal detector, but once he approached the check-in counter, Czech passport in hand, his stomach sank.

"Where are you headed?" asked the airline employee.

"Netherlands."

"Please wait here. Five minutes."

Ahmad watched other passengers admitted through check in. He approached the desk once more. "What about me?" he asked.

"Five more minutes," came the answer.

"Okay."

Two policemen appeared. Ahmad looked up at them approaching. They stopped in front of him.

"Hey," one said. "Where are you from?"

"Czech Republic."

"You sure? Where are you really from—Syria or Iraq?"

"No. Czech."

"You're coming upstairs with us. You're gonna tell us where you're from."

"Okay! Okay. Syria."

They took his bag. They took the passport. They called him bad words, and kicked him out.

Ahmad's first call was to Ali. "The police caught me. I didn't make it."

"Don't worry," came Ali's familiar refrain. "You'll go tomorrow. Wait for me to get a new passport for you."

Ahmad actually waited three days for the new papers, not one. This one said he was Danish, and the ticket was to Milan.

At this point I laugh aloud. Ahmad looks like he could credibly be from about half the world's countries, but I wouldn't say Denmark is among them. He offers up another one of his wry smiles.

"What a circus," I say.

"I said to Ali," Ahmad agrees, "I say to Ali, 'Ali, I don't think—"

"You'll reach the Netherlands," Ali said definitively. "I've done this with a hundred people. I'm a professional. This is my job. Respect my job. Wait. I'll send you a new one."

Ahmad went from Athens to Crete's airport, but still was not surprised when that one didn't work, and he once again called Ali. The next passport to show up was Italian, but that still didn't do the trick. Ahmad was once again kicked out of the airport.

After the Czech, Danish, and Italian passports all didn't work, Ali bid Ahmad come back to Athens. "We'll figure out how to get you out," he said, "from one of the other islands. I think Santorini will be better. That might work."

It was a forty-five euro trip on ship to Crete, then back again to Athens. Ahmad was out another hundred euros, "and with zero dream," he says to me.

After the latest trip to Athens, which took another seventeen hours, Ahmad was feeling truly despondent. He spent three days walking around, and didn't hear from Ali. So, he went to a hookah bar, one of those places with music and hashish. One of those places where you order coffee, but don't actually want any. One of those places where you whisper to the waiter that you're Syrian, and you need help. One of those places where the waiter disappears and the music and dancing keep filling up the space along with the sweet smoke. One of those places where "five thousand euros" is again the magic number.

"Where do I pay it?"

"There's an office."

"Okay. How long do I have to wait?"

"Two or three days. Do you have a picture?"

"Yes."

"Give it to me. Actually, you need a new one. Call this number tomorrow, when you've got the new photo."

The man at the other end of that phone call was named Mahmoud. "We need an interview," he told Ahmad. "We can meet at that same cafe."

Three days later, Mahmoud presented Ahmad with a Bulgarian passport. "You leave tomorrow morning," he said.

Ahmad pauses to explain to me that Greece has around two hundred small airports during the months between May and September, to service the vacationing Europeans who want to summer on the villas without the hassle of stopping through Athens. If you could convince the authorities you're one of those Europeans, you could get on one of the flights from a small Greek airport to a big European country. But it needed to be in the summer months. Says Ahmad: "This is the golden time to pass."

So Ahmad went to Santorini. "Very wonderful place," he recalls. He got a load of how small the airport was, and hope returned to his chest.

At the Santorini airport on the day of the flight he hoped to catch, the airline employee asked Ahmad for his nationality.

"Bulgarian," he said.

"Liar," came the answer. "I've got a Bulgarian friend just here. Maybe you can speak with him, to prove you're not lying."

Ahmad, of course, could not, and the airport police threw him out. He was down nearly one hundred euro again. "It was a very bad experience," he says with finality.

Ahmad crosses the kitchen and comes close to me as I sit against the wall at his little table.

"Identify," he says.

It takes me a moment to realize he's acting out his experience at the airport. I fish around for my passport and he looks at it, then up at me, then down at the passport again. He explains that if he'd looked even 70% like the photo in the passport, he'd have tried to pass through Greece with it.

"Don't people report them stolen?" I ask.

"In Athens you can do everything," he answers, which I take to mean that the black market is bustling. But in spite of his effort to hustle, alongside and against Tunisians, Egyptians, Somalians, Sudanese, and other Syrians, he didn't succeed.

"Finally," he says, "I decide to go by—" he taps his phone—"truck. To

Spain." He gets up from his seat and sits alongside me, only lower: he slides down the wall until he sits on his kitchen floor.

4,500 euros later, Ahmad found himself squeezed between bags, unable to get up or walk for a total of thirty-two hours, during which he couldn't move, walk, stand, smoke, use his phone, eat, or urinate. After five hours the truck went into port, boarded a ship, and after another five hours of driving until he and the other the fifteen stowaways were released into an Italian orchard under cover of night.

"Go! Go! Go!" said the driver in the dark, hurrying them on with motions of his hand.

The first thing Ahmad did, in a garden by the highway, was tear up his *kharziya*, just as Ali had taught him. Then he followed the highway for six kilometers, tired, hungry, and frightened the authorities would catch him. He feared the Italians' taking his fingerprint, knowing that once they got it, he would not reach his dream of school and an apartment. He had one hundred euros to get to Milan. First he arrived at a small bus station, and bought the espresso and tobacco he so craved. As they filled his system, he forgot about his anger, his aches and pains. He called to let Ali know that Ali could pick his money up. Ali was businesslike about it; he didn't care how Ahmad was feeling and didn't ask after his health or his family. He wanted Ahmad's money. Ahmad had been a job and that job was finished.

Ahmad asked at the little window about trains to Milan. There was one leaving in three hours, and the trip itself would cost fifty-six euros and take another ten hours.

In a way, I think, being a refugee trying not to get caught is a lethally high-stakes version of an auditioning actor who never got a break: Ahmad was always working, always on, even after forty wakeful and cramped hours and miles of road under his feet, he was here in another country that didn't want him. His duties were clear: get a ticket, be silent, wait, be calm, don't speak with anyone you don't know, sleep if you can, don't make sudden movements, lest the police catch you. If police catch you, they'll take your fingerprint, and that, in Ahmad's words, is "the end of your dream."

When he arrived in Milan's Central Station, he had an address: a place on Via Antonio, a place that helped Syrian people. "They said owner of this is Jewish," Ahmad says, tapping the ash off his cigarette. "They say. I don't know." He was fed there three times a day, and given a clean bed to sleep in until his departure from Milan. Now, he'd need to decide on his final destination.

CHAPTER V

In Italy, there were two ways to do what Ahmad calls "continue the dream:" to depart Italy from the Leonardo da Vinci International Airport or to go by private taxi and then train. Italian identity papers cost 150 euros, and a ticket from Milan to Stockholm was another 200. Ahmad was by now afraid of the airport police, after being kicked out of Greek airports so many times. He opted for a private taxi. To get to the Netherlands, Ahmad would need to find a taxi that would go through France and Belgium. To get to Denmark, Sweden, Norway, or Finland, his taxi would go through Austria, and Germany. To get to France or Austria costs 350 euros; to get to Belgium, Germany, Denmark, or the Netherlands the journey would cost 550. Ahmad would need to pay half the price before the taxi trip, and the other half once he arrived.

The most dangerous part of the trip would be between Salzburg, Austria, and Copenhagen, Denmark. Ahmad had heard that if you're caught by Austrian police, they'd turn you over to the German police, and no Arab person wanted that. "But now," he points out, "all Arabian people prefer Germany because of Angela Merkel."

Ahmad looks up at me and sees the question in my expression. "Because Merkel respects Arabian people," he explains. "Give Arabian people rights. Respect Muslim people and"—he taps something out on his phone to translate—"*strongly sympathizes* with them."

"We respect prime minister. If you ask me, I respect Hillary Clinton. If you ask me, I don't respect Obama. We respect who strongly sympathizes with us. I respect Abraham Lincoln."

Ahmad rubs his chest. He is disheveled and his chest hurts from a fist fight he got into the other day with his brother, the one who is also in Sweden.

"What's going on there, man?" I ask.

"I go Monday to make X-ray," he says.

He sees me looking, and wanting to say more. "You don't know what happened," he says.

"That's true, I allow, "I don't. But you could tell me. Is it your chest?"

"It's my leg, my chest."

"Maybe he bruised your ribs," I say.

"In Milan," Ahmad says with a heavy sign, "you have to ask about man who has taxi."

He found one named Mustafa, another Egyptian—or a phone number for him, anyway. He gave Mustafa the same details that profiled him to the string of countries that looked to kick him out: he was a Syrian, a refugee, and he needed to get somewhere else.

"Where are you?" Mustafa's voice crackled over the phone.

"Milan."

"Wait there. We'll pick you up in two hours. Got any money?"

"Yes."

"How much to you have?"

"How much do you need?"

"Well, where do you want to go?"

"The Netherlands."

"Can't do that. My driver to the Netherlands was arrested. He's in prison. France has his fingerprints. They have the fingerprints of everyone who was with him. How about Sweden?"

"All right."

"You'll need to take either a taxi or a flight to Denmark."

"No flights. I know about airports. I'm not doing that again."

The magic number Mustafa quoted was 750 euros. If Ahmad had that, then he needed to be ready to leave before dawn along with five others like him. His destination would be Sweden, he decided; so he'd ride until Denmark, at which point a train would take him from Copenhagen to the first stop in Sweden.

Ahmad's family sent him 850 euros. The 100 leftover would get him from Copenhagen to Malmö. There in Milan he got the funds his family sent with his Syrian passport, and headed to the hotel Mustafa told him about. The driver of Mustafa's private cab, Ahmad tells me, was like a prime minister, or a businessman! A driver in the Arabian world, in India, they're tired and haggard. Not this one. This one looked like a gentleman. The car was nice, Italian, and he played nice music. There was nothing about the car or driver to raise the suspicion of the police.

The slick driver cautioned them that they were still on the job: no talking, no smoking, no sudden movements.

They made it the two hours from Italy to Austria. They made it the nine hours from Austria to Germany. No police stopped them or asked for their papers. The gentleman driver did not speed. Ahmad and his fellow passengers were allowed to eat snacks. They'd occasionally make a pit stop, and the driver would call them back from where they pissed behind the bushes with a clap of his hands.

The eleven hours through Germany to Denmark were especially terrifying for Ahmad, with everything he'd heard about German police. "Please, please stay calm," the gentleman driver begged. "Please don't make a sound. If they catch me, I'm done for. I'll lose the car and go to prison for ten years, and you'll lose your dream."

But they made it. They made it the eleven hours from Germany to Denmark. "Get free, man," says Ahmad, mimicking the driver, collecting the second half of their fee and shaking each of them by the hand: "Congratulations. You'll get your dream."

Ahmad and a couple of the others got food at an Arabian café in the train station in Copenhagen. They took their tickets from a ticket machine. It was a twenty-minute ride that cost eight euro. Ahmad set foot in Malmö at one in the morning. He'd stayed in Istanbul for a month; in Izmir for a month; in Myteline for four days; in Greece for ten months, and Milan for ten days.

Only now does Ahmad tell me what happened after his kharziya ran out in Greece: once his six months were up, he'd been arrested. He'd been beaten by police, and stuck in a Greek jail. He spent eight days in that jail. It was a bad, bad jail. Ahmad repeats over and over: "A very, very, very, very, very bad experience. Very bad experience. Very bad police."

Greek police were like Syrian police. They beat him like Assad's people had. Ahmad remembers it was one of the worst experiences of his life: "the same pain." He saw people in there from Ghana, Nigeria, Pakistan, Afghanistan, Egypt, Tunisia, Morocco. They dreamt about Italy, Ahmad says, the way Syrians dreamt about Sweden or the Netherlands. Ahmad emerged, beaten and bruised, with a new *kharziya*. An Algerian guy had stolen his phone.

"Is it good for you?" he gestures to my phone, recording his voice. Outside the sunlight has become the color of honey; my bus is leaving soon.

"No," I say. He'd arrived in Sweden fifteen months ago. "I want to know the rest of the story."

CHAPTER VI

When Ahmad got to Malmö, he waited in the train station until morning. It was very cold. He went to where all Syrians go when they get to Sweden: the immigrant processing center in Arlöv. He presented himself as he truly was: a Syrian. He gave them his real papers. He gave them his fingerprints and stood for a photo. They gave him a room with a bed and central heating.

Even Syrians didn't respect him the way Swedes did, he tells me. He gets up to illustrate how he learned the difference between Swedish people and Syrian people, hurrying to the tap, filling the water glass—"What you need?" he asks me in a fakely high voice, "Water? Here are you!"—that he was accepted, that he was respected: after all he'd been through, Ahmad had trouble believing it.

He spent six months in the forest, in Alstermo, where it was often below fifteen degrees outside. He couldn't study or anything like that, not yet. He didn't know where the Swedish government would send him. He's an excitable, sensitive, intelligent guy, a young lawyer; even though he needed to recover for a while, six months was a long stretch of time for him to have nothing to do. It wasn't even in a town—his building was in the forest. His roommates were three Syrians—one from Latakia, one from Damascus, one from Aleppo—and a Palestinian. The 2,800 Swedish kronor he got every month was just enough for food, drink, cigarettes, and a cell phone. He spent the whole time finding an apartment, because once you do that, he tells me, you can present the Swedish government with your new address, and they'll give you rights.

In the middle of October, Ahmad moved to this apartment in a village near Karlstad. The Swedish government gave him membership at a bank, and identity documents. This village, also, is like a forest, he jokes wryly: no one talks to him here, either.

His Swedish teacher does, though. Nina, his Swedish "Mother Teresa," who is his sister, mother, father, brother, and mentor all at once. He is a very bright student, she tells him, with a bright future. When he tells her his stories, she weeps.

It's not that Swedish people aren't kind, he says quickly; they're very kind, but also reserved, as if they're afraid he's a terrorist.

*

"Someone needs money." That's how Ahmad explains the theft of his mobile phone. He knows the pickpockets in Greece, in Italy, have no better way to make a living. He knows that many are, like him, "migrants" and unwanted. "He didn't pay for it," Ahmad reasons, "so he can sell it for any price."

The afternoon has waned as our interview stretched into its fourth hour. My bus leaves soon, from the roundabout a few blocks away. I'll make my way back to Stockholm, the yellow express train whipping through verdant summer fields. Ahmad is tired. Bone-tired. Soul tired. He mentions Obama again: the Syrian people don't need money or food from people, he insists; they need Assad to be driven out. If the American people vote Obama out, Obama will go. That's how government is supposed to work in America, and that's what Syrians want. It's why there were peaceful protests in the first place, in the Spring of 2011.

"Obama respects what people want," Ahmad affirms. He's getting to the tail end of his umpteenth cigarette. "Like Angela Merkel. Like any prime minister or president. People say, 'Please go out, we don't need you,' he respects and go out. Like Sarkozy. We are Arabian people like you. We don't need Bashar Assad. When we say 'We don't need you', they use bombs, they kill us, more than 200 killing every day—I can show you picture—"

"I've seen pictures," I say quickly.

Instead he shows me a video of himself leading a peaceful demonstration of lawyers in Aleppo. In it, he cries out that every Syrian child is his child, and that Syrians of all religions are family because they are Syrian. Those sorts of demonstrations are what got him arrested three times: once for eight hours, once for fifteen days ("the hardest," he says), and the last for an amount of time he doesn't specify. He left immediately after that. Someone paid to get him out. Someone who cared about him. Someone who told him: "They will kill you. You are dangerous. Do you know what it is you did? You stood up and said you needed freedom. Bashar Assad doesn't accept that."

Ahmad is sure of this: Bashar Assad is not Barack Obama. Assad expects you to weep and pray at his feet, to lick his shoes. Assad expects that you'll break in front of him. "Say nice words," Ahmad tells me. "Not like American anti, Left, Right, radical, no. All Syrians are Bashar Assad's. Bashar Assad will give you water, he will give you internet, he will give you electricity, he will give you phones, and then he will take. Bashar Assad can kill you or let you alive."

I am silent in the face of this, sitting across from him. I stare at the crumbs left by the cookies of his that I've gobbled up. I don't know what else there could be to say. It's 2015 and it has long been the case that there is no comfort for Syrians. It is perhaps wrong to act as if there is.

"Bashar Assad can do everything with Iran," Ahmad continues. "Iran is Shia, okay, and dream to control all Muslim people. From Lebanon with Hezbollah, til Syria with Shia Assad, til Bahrain, with Shia also: Iran dreams to control all Muslim countries and make them educated with Shia way. There is difference between Catholic and Protestant or Orthodox: difference between Shia and Sunni. All Muslim but they're different. I think with this way, they think the other way, okay. Our message is: we have right to live safe. We have right to see our child grow up with a good life. We are all Syrian, we are not Muslim Christian, Muslim Sunni, Muslim Shia, Arabian, no we are all Syrian. We need freedom. We need freedom. We need freedom. We don't need to lost our young child in your bad army. You take young child and you teach him to kill his brother. You are really bad one ever. Stop. Go out. We need freedom."

"Do you understand?" he asks me. "Do you believe?"

He holds out a picture. "This is sick old man. Water on his shoulder. He takes water on shoulder in Syria now. No internet in Syria now. Just Bashar Assad. And Free Army, and Da'ish."

He returns to Hillary Clinton, who, as Secretary of State—here he gets up, once again to act out, but it's not his own story this time: he stands erect, as if at a podium. "Bashar Assad," he thunders, "you must go." Then he claps, miming the impressed audience.

*

75

But Bashar Assad hasn't, and in the time since I spent that afternoon in that Swedish village, watching Ahmad's tired face, he hasn't. He didn't as Ahmad spent the requisite month in Malmö's immigrant processing center in early 2014, living in an apartment with only the forest, waiting for the Swedish government to tell him where he would spend his days, where he would go to school.

"What about your siblings?" I ask, bracing myself to pay close attention, pen at the ready, to try and keep track of the many people in Ahmad's immediate family.

Ahmad's sister Raghad, who has four children, lost her husband to Assad's bombs. She lives with another sister, Ahed, in Lebanon. Another sister, Nawal, lost her husband to one of Putin's bombs, and still lives in Syria with her two children. His sister Reem's husband was injured by a sniper in early 2016. His brother Issa is in Izmir, Turkey. A little brother, Mousa, is in Germany. Mohamed, with whom he had the fistfight, moved to Sweden also, a few months after Ahmad. His wife and child remain in Turkey, waiting to join him.

His father is dead. His sister is dead. His mother lives alone in a bad apartment and Ahmad sends her around 100 euro every month. She is terribly ill with heart disease and diabetes, but she still went from Turkey *back into* Syria to pluck her youngest son, Musab, from the ranks of Da'ish, with whom teenage Musab had enlisted.

("Wait," I say, smiling in spite of myself, "Your mother was very, very ill, but she *returned to Syria* to bring her teenage son home? I like your mother."

"My mother is strong one," Ahmad solemnly agrees. "My mother like mountain.")

An uncle brought Musab to Germany. They hope Musab can now bring their mother, who could use the medical care, because Musab is still underage. As Ahmad is not, he can't bring her to Sweden. His fiancée, Ranim, is in Aleppo; the Swedish government, as of early 2016, has permitted her to travel to Sweden.

His last words of the interview: "I feel alone. I feel nostalgia for everyone. I feel alone. Mother, father, sister, brother: you have just a mobile to know everything about everything. Just study. Feel bad sometimes. Sometimes energy come, sometimes energy go. I think all the Syrian people feel so. I hope I can bring my family. I hope I can see freedom in my country. I hope I can see Assad go out. I hope I can see like American people like every good people. I hope no one loses member of his family, no one loses feeling by army. Every day I think about everything. Ranim lives in Aleppo with her family, under Bashar Assad control. I think more about all of them. It's not just names. My sister. My brother. I look like... look tired under my eyes, my body, smoke more, eat less, sleep less. I'm going to doctors here. They talked with me about my... but cannot find answers to my questions. When I say I need my sister, they say Swedish law can't give you this right. When I say I need my wife, they say you wait. You must wait for 18 months. Just if you... to be like crazy. To get mad. Story of my family."

EPILOGUE

Winter 2016: I come back to the office I share with three other graduate students, after teaching at a California university by the ocean, to a Whatsapp voice message from Ahmad. Three of them, actually. In all of them, he is weeping. His brother-in-law died. I stare at a postcard of a girl on a swing tacked to the wall above my desk, hearing the gravel in Ahmad's voice. It's the dead of night where he is. His profile picture is now his lost brother-in-law. He sends me a picture of his now-fatherless nephew, who is two.

Outside my office, I can hear the surf. I can't see the ocean from here, but I can hear it. It's rhythmic and low, like Ahmad's voice when he sends me little videos on Whatsapp to explain how he likes to eat his *zaatar*. It's rhythmic and low, an ocean of unplumbable depths. Faint like the photoslide in a daylit room, where lost loved ones hover on the edge of one's vision. The growl of absence that accompanies the solitude of anyone who has loved and lost. I keep thinking of Ahmad's explanation of Ramadan: that it's about understanding hunger, which makes you compassionate for those who go hungry, and dwelling with the pain of absence. That it's not about how cool and lethargic you feel without what you need, lingering in the dry desert heat, but about the intimate crawl of sunset, spreading across the wide sky, and the food emerging from the kitchen that you've waited for like you wait for your sweetheart to come home: the sensuous joy of finally getting what you wait for.

Maine, USA

TYPEWRITER

Thru the glass

With the ripple in it, past the sill

Which is dusty—If there is someone
In the garden!
Outside, and so beautiful.

—*from* "Image of the Engine," George Oppen

1976.

Summer evening, Hill House porch, Eagle Island, Maine.

George, Mary and Helene talk of something philosophical.

Helene stuffs a chicken. George lights a match for his pipe.

Tractor rests in sunlight.

And there, northeast of the outhouse, a triangle of ocean so blue

it startles you.

I.

I plant spinach with Helene, ocean on either side. Bob's tractor sends up dandelion seeds. My head on Helene's lap, on a couch, in the back of a lobster boat. We feel like queens on top of the protective plastic wrapping. Dirt under nails.

I listen to a book on tape as my mother does habitually. I slide into being her as we putter in gardens on separate coasts. We talk more often now, about once a month, and her voice comes in round shapes. I think spherical is glad.

Before and after taking the mail boat out to the island it is a tradition for me to stay in a roomy white bed in the roomy white house of a woman, Mindy, who met my mother in a college dorm in Oregon forty years ago. They hit it off immediately, downed a case of beer, Mindy's dark hair already striped with white, my mother intelligent and stunning. We were very philosophical, says Mindy.

I remember this wandering at low tide: mollusk-ridden ridges. Plucking not one snail from the conglomeration of them. In blue soup with water and seaweed, those bubbles one can pop. A cold day in early June. Time bends. The rock is striped. Possible to read rocks for age, for events in their history. Life happened to my mother and Mindy; they correspond rarely. Forty years is but a trifle. Fire in grate thrums. Rain streaks. I have only ever known Mindy with hair pale and light as petals. I shook-shook a carrot with a peeler. Marked already by what is about to happen, by how life-gravity draws to place where hands deftly employ tools fashioned from sky, metal, regret. On the piano, pictures in frames. The tide is low. The moon is pulling.

The submerging is easy.

II.

I handle tender seedlings, ocean wherever I glance up. The garden-way cart has lost its back panel. A candle flickers on the dining room table, set for supper, Bob's favorite spoon where it should be. The island groans as the wind kicks up. Full of Helene's poppyseed muffins and skinned-kneed, I'd stare at the attic window, sure a pale woman would appear there, looking back.

For here ghosts are loosened.

The air upsets across open meadow and perplexes them into ruffling, acting. Helene never specifies when we ask her if anyone died in the farmhouse, in the attic rooms where we, her dish-washing, odd-job-doing "summer daughters," sleep and hang stray pieces of frilled linen over the rafters.

But if there *are* ghosts, she says carefully, they manifest themselves as a benevolent presence.

The here-and-there baby sunflower plants must be moved to the north corner of the garden. What if we are G-d's playthings indeed, his trinkets, his pendants? Earrings his mother left behind and loved, living in the smooth wood box. The box that never lost its rose-water smell. I loosen dirt with fingers that morph, wizen then soften, and the scent of dirt is then loosened in plumes and the worms loosened in violet haste, arching.

My mother calls hens "biddies." Bob has built a handy sliding door with a nail or two and a board for collecting eggs. The biddies eat table scraps and line up like pumpkins when light falls away along the edge of the planet. "I'm learning to invite my daydreams in for chats," I write. The blackness of night is not the blackest there is. Nor of soil.

What forces work on that patch of ocean to lighten it so? Not sun, just. The flies group on that side of the rock for a reason. I take a walk after the morning routine to a currently tenant-less cottage called Little Camp, lie on top of the scratchy wool blankets. I look up from a book and between mothballs a sound like music swells with a heavy thing, a thing like love, unbalanced, webbed and diagonal. Outside things are ebbing.

Bleeding is supposed to be the loss of something.

Sara, another summer daughter, cuts my hair. Helene has gone ashore, so we are to act as satellites around the radio in case Bob needs something. Karl, a summer son, clicks the Rubix cube into place again. This is heaven, I think. This moment lives on. Sometime soon we will make cocoa. I am thinking of basil, and of participation. I scribble in my journal: "Isn't participation in a moment the biggest thanks I can give for its arrival? And what about widening what that means? How can a daydream be outside of that if, during a moment, one daydreams?"

This rain might wash away the seeds.

III.

Look.
Look at all you've
Forgotten.

Red top-grass. A black crow lining over billowing laundry. The pieces of your life, the ones reflected in the wiggling glass, the cracked glass—here where she digs mollusk shells from the compost heap that baby radishes might grow unhindered.

The summer you began to garden, the summer you again picked up your paintbrush.

She is thrilled I fit into her old clothes, the ones she saved. In the warmth of the attic my belly morphs with time's erratic twinges, bulkens, softens after birth.

He was a fine sailor, is the first thing Bob has to say about George. Bob knows a number of sailors and does not say this about many of them—any of them, to my knowledge.

Next he says: he was on the fringes of keeping bad company.

Then heads out the door, slanted forward not with age but with purpose, to fix the propane tank.

Helene turns to me, wiping hands on apron, explains: He hung out with Ezra Pound. In France. He and Mary drifted, went to Mexico. Bob, home for dinner and accosted by me on the couch, puts down the paper and says, they were like hippies but too early to be hippies. Bohemian, I think they were called.

One kind of night everyone loves: foggy, when candles are lit and Bob is persuaded to read rhyming, rhythmic poetry written by Robert Quin, Sr., and kept in an aging binder. His voice, and that of Helene, cradled by Down East accent, sounds itself like a prow through dark water, a rich growl.

IV.

The word I keep hearing from Bob, Helene, and their daughter Treena is *gentle*. They were gentle people, George and Mary. Helene pauses: highly evolved intellect. They went where the wind took them, loved their boat. Went, G-d knows why, way-the-hell-and-gone out to Matinicus—the farthest islet in the chain out from Deer Isle. Bob shakes his head about this in the same way he shook his head at that fact that I have been to Siberia. Bob knows his rock, knows it very well, stays there if he can. Couldn't go out in storms because their boat was small and George and Mary were small too, wind would've knocked 'em clean over.

Bob stayed on Eagle even after all of his siblings left, said get off that rock, Bob, go have a life somewhere. One day when I was thirteen Bob and I walked through the wood up to the farmhouse. I asked him what he did after high school. Bob served in the army. I learned how to shoot people, he said, and didn't have much to say beyond that. Naturally he came right back to Eagle when it was over. On the way through the woods he pointed at a Maine Forest Association sign and indicated unhappiness at a mark made on it by a rock someone had thrown.

What I can't stop thinking after Helene mentions that a poet came to Eagle summers of the 70's, after she says he was named George Oppen, after she tells me that the typewriter he used and other things of his and his wife Mary's are in the Hill House attic, after I am shocked that no one has ever wanted to go see them, after I find the key to the attic on the crowded ring that hangs next to the outgoing mail basket in the farmhouse, after I arrange to do the dinner dishes so as to have the afternoon off and daylight to see by, after I struggle with the door in the floor of the attic and heave myself up into its must and close heat and mouse shit and toys and clothes from the 70's, after I realize that little light makes it in here anyway, what I can't stop thinking is: is this anyone's to unearth?

A Gulf of Maine map covers the top of a box bearing the markered label: "clothes: G & M."

Between a rusted stove and a pile of 2x4s, something over which is draped a blue, polyester shirt covered in red paisleys.

It is gray. It says "Royal." The Y, V, G, and H keys are stuck down.
I hit the tab button.
It rings.
Breezes sneak up the eaves.

1976.

Summer evening, Hill House porch, Eagle Island, Maine.

George, Mary, and Helene talk of something philosophical.

Helene stuffs a chicken. George lights a match for his pipe,

Succumbs just then to consideration of topic, holds lit match.

The fringes of the tablecloth catch fire.

"We laughed about that one for a long time."

The books left behind by George and Mary, in order of their stacked-ness as I lifted them one by one out of the box: *The Education of Henry Adams*. Virgil: *The Pastoral Poems. Basic Readings from the Kabbalah*. Woolf: *Between the Acts, Jacob's Room, Letters of, Night and Day, The Death of the Moth, To the Lighthouse, The Waves*. Koestler: *Dialogue With Death*. Maritain: *Existence and the Existent: an Essay on Christian Existentialism*. Brod: *Franz Kafka Biography. Euripides III. Aeschylus I*. Adams: *The United Sates in 1800*. Heidegger: *An Introduction to Metaphysics*. Jeffers: *The Women of Big Sur and Other Poems*. Helman: *Scoundrel Time. The Canterbury Tales*. Brown: *The United States and India, Pakistan, and Bangladesh*. Sayers: *Gaudy Night*. Bancroft: *The Life of Washington*. Polk: *The United States and the Arab World*.

All the words I could make out from George's notes in the soft book cover of Heidegger's *An Introduction to Metaphysics*:

> *"...what has not been known. No one can help him, nothing can appease him. He was no gentleman & no kindness at all-.*
>
> *If we can ask...and knock,*
> *we...it is not home.*
> *(Bugs?) could mean the fury of (walden?) and*
> *His king of eternity.*

...of nothingness
fear of finding
Nothingness

the garden of what mass is
must always be taken in its
existential.................
stands with being.

... anyone
can be secure w order
Because.........order,
It cannot contain us.

As we wanted
Knowledge.

Oh, my will...Tails, tennis balls...walk!

"This is where" all truth is contained.
-the universe contains all truth-

...and fearful

it cannot be mastered
we are strange for we lose
the strangeness of death

if a man...full
fledged and alone
...the universe—
what would he feel?
What would he see? How would
He understand it?"

Same, for George's notes in the margins of Maritain's *Existence and the Existent*:

> *"The act of existence is*
> *the fact of*
> *being material. The*
> *problem of metaphysics*
> *is the existence of*
> *matter..."*
>
> *Eastern mystic...:*
> *...moral tragedy.*
>
> *Unlike...,*
> *...moral*
> *tragedy is*
> *<u>denied</u>. Man as an historical being is himself.*
>
> *And if it*
> *Exactly...*
>
> *The statement, in...*
> *Is valid*
> *true*
>
> *...creates nothing new,*
> *...gives realness to the real"*

V.

The many islands constituting this part of Maine's unorganized territory boast two official year-long residents. Bob and Helene Quinn both come from families whose involvement with Eagle, a mile-by-half-mile swatch of land just off Deer Isle in the Penobscot Bay, goes back for generations. Bob went to school on the island in the white schoolhouse that people can still visit if they borrow the key with the bell attached from the farmhouse kitchen. The chalkboard is covered in signatures, and the maps are comically outdated. Most of Bob's family is buried on Eagle in a small cemetery down the road from Haeni's Beach, where fake flowers garnish white, moss-covered stone. Only one road goes down the middle of the island, and it's called Highway 1. And what I mean when I say it's called that is that people call it that, some people, with a smile in their throats.

Helene meets my mother while my mother is living with my half-sister in Blue Hill. My mother, Blue Hill Hospital's first alcohol counselor, has advertised at Stonington High for a talk-to-your-youth-about-alcohol meeting. Helene, who works at the high school and has a youth (Treena), is one of the only four people to show up. They all troop back to someone's place for tea. Fifteen years after that I see the island for the first time. Five years after *that* I return alone to "work" for Helene and Bob, and do so for the next six summers and counting.

The Oppens are doing their perfunctory exploring when Bob finds them on his island around 1970. A fan of George's on the mainland has been a little too ever-present even for the kind and open-hearted Oppens, so the Oppens have sailed on, looking for a quieter spot. The Oppens stay on Eagle. Bob isn't much for the kind of poetry George writes and has just won a Pulitzer for. The Quinns and the Oppens cherish the company they find in each other, and it isn't poetry they talk about.

Very worthwhile people, says either Helene or Bob retrospectively. One of them says it right at the time sharp sunlight filters into the dining room to slice candlesticks and glass. I don't remember which one says it. It is something either one would say.

Big Camp, a red cabin on the west side of the Island where a Swedish seamstress now stays every summer, didn't used to be red. I don't know what else about it was different when the Oppens called it home each summer. For however long it was their home, for whatever conditions made something home for them. By all accounts, the Oppens' home was in each other. By all accounts, moving from place to place helps one to locate a space, a home inside oneself. By all accounts, the Quinns travel rarely. But by all accounts, the Quinns are at home.

I walk to Big Camp at sunset on my last day on Eagle summer 2004. Every summer I forget about the thorns in Big Camp's yard and wander there barefoot. Big Camp is locked, just a modest three-room cabin catching the best of the dying light. There is a 1968 car, rusting between Big Camp and Little Camp. Little Camp is the neighboring cottage I used to sneak into to read. As it turns out, the Oppens would put up their guests there. The guests were often literary types and fans. Before and after entertaining them, recalls either Bob or Helene, and between random stretches of days when boat and crew would disappear, the two small adventurers would return, walk up to the farmhouse, waving.

VI.

Sometimes we go ashore. Typically it is to grocery shop. Flour, milk, tomatoes. Helene's informal Eagle Island Bakery has been a hit with people staying on Eagle, Barred, Great Spruce, etc. One thing I have done a few times is pick my way down the path to the shore slowly, holding a package in my hands firmly horizontal so as not to disturb the pie.

Sometimes Bob delivers, say, still-warm Anadama bread over to, say, Great Spruce Head and lets me lie on my stomach on the nose of his boat, TMII, staring at the churning white, glancing up to look for seals. I'm terrible at knotting rope, though Bob tries many times to show me, looping it around a spoke of the steering wheel, then undoing it for me to try. Bob carries the deep smell of lobster bait in with him at the end of the day. His lobster traps are furnished with buoys painted orange and black.

The path down to the shore is the same one Bob takes every day to his boat, and I have been with him as he stops and takes a gander at the view, the view that only for him and Helene is not a rare one. Not showily. Just looks.

Bob's last boat, the Treena Marie, was named after his daughter. It was totaled in a storm some years back. Helene described it once. Bob sensed what happened to his boat before they made it down to the shore. He could just tell.

Bob is having trouble with his teeth lately. It rankles him. Helene cooks up a lot of yams, boils vegetables until they are soft, prepares tender fish. A good guy, Helene says about him once as I sweep the kitchen floor. I have just asked her how does someone know when someone is right for them, and she has boiled it down to whether you would feel okay taking care of them when they are sick. That's not all of it, she says, but a necessary part.

Julia, another summer daughter, asks Bob once if he has any regrets. The only one he comes up with is keeping Helene from traveling due to his homebodiness. He knows she loves to travel.

This summer I nap in the car while Bob and Helene do errands in Brewer. The inside of the little Swedish car is a yellowish brown. It is *hot*. When they get back, Bob reminds me to sit up for the car ride part because he could be fined $60. They've just been to see their accountant.

Bob explains things in terms like "inheritance" and "entitlement," but I can't understand on account of the lump in my throat. I've just learned what "eminent domain" means, Bob and Helene settle on a restaurant and inside it is beautifully cool. Helene asks what I'll have and I think maybe just an appetizer. She straightens, her brown curls lifted with hours of heat. Don't order something just because it costs less, she says, you get whatever you want. Bob agrees. He is in his customary button-up plaid shirt, glasses clean, eyes twinkling. Helene beside him in a striped cotton tee from Reny's. Just warning you, I'm going to give you some money before you go to Boston, she says. You don't have any money to give, I protest, I work for room and board. I have more money than you do, she says. This is the first day, alone with Bob and Helene away from the business of the island, that I know to ask harder questions. I have never heard Bob speak in terms of meaning. It's simple. The meaning of the island to him outweighs the financial hardship of living there. The same goes for Helene. We could be millionaires if we wanted, Helene says. I glance up quickly: they look different to me. Sitting together. Spectacles gleaming. They could if they wanted, but they don't. Side by side.

VII.

A stethoscope.

Wet-weather gear smelling of bird shit.

"Desk Materials: G & M"

Empty used manila envelopes, most addressed to the Oppens on Eagle. On 7/25/77 someone sent George a manuscript to look over from Blue Bird Press, called "Night Shift" by a Maria Someone. A can of smoking tobacco. A postcard or two from 1977. All well, how are you, etc. Can't read name of sender. I begin to feel strange. My hands are separate from me, sorting through inky shrapnel. Looking at them sift through someone else's things, I think, those can't be mine. The things. The hands.

At the bottom of the box, one piece of yellow legal pad paper, folded. On the bottom half is written:

> *Sometimes I cannot move at all and will not either*
>
> *I imagine myself looking over a group of hills*
>
> *The trees begin*
> *begin to sway and*
> *as I watch I Turn*
> *Turn   Turn inward*
> *And outward toward myself toward myself standing*
> *Standing in entrances————-about to come in. When*
> *when am I going to enter?*
>
> *Come in   come in   I say to all the fragment**
> [Rachel Blau DuPlessis]

(written in pen; a graphite pencil line drawn across the page as if to discard it) Helene recognizes Mary's handwriting.

Jan 3 1981

Dear Helene,

We are both well. George
is having trouble remembering—
This problem of <u>age</u> is hard to
place, hard to accept, hard to
understand. We are together which
is most important to us both—
almost all activity & decisions
devolve on me, this again
is hard on George who has been
forced to give up & give up
and give up—perfectly
conscious of his loss.
We will be here when
 you come—a long time or
 a short—just let us
know the dates. We have
<u>two</u> rooms for you—and
we will talk. We'll show
off San Francisco, of course
also.
 Love to you all
we think of you so often, as
though time had not elapsed—

Mary

A family friend called Sally visits Mary at her house in Berkeley in 1989 and sends a report and photos back to Helene. *We spoke of you a lot.* One of the photos is of a painting Mary did on Eagle of the view. It stands on her mantelpiece.

Has decided with her doctor to continue therapy as needed to "contain" the cancer...behind her house she has a vegetable and flower garden—she has to work on it very slowly, a little at a time. Now it has been put to bed. She said she found narcissus blooming! She never knew they were there.

Only can say: I am unearthing something about the sixth sense. What it senses.

In the red grassy field where children have played tag every summer for a century I see silhouettes, light pulsing.

Even in the photos, in old age, Mary's eyes hasten blue.

After leaving the Island I read the 1975 George Oppen issue of *Ironwood 5;* Mary's memoir, *Meaning a Life,* and *The Materials,* on July days riding the subway to and from Russian class, marveling at the people, the words, the starts and stops, my first time living in a city, and alone, too. Sweat. Words. Sticking. I duck my head, read, look up.

It's not that this does nothing. It's that I double back, try to do it properly. Research.

No use. Before I even try to read a bibliography: the deed, or damage, is done. These were the Oppens I met.

Not mine to think, sifting through sweaters, undergarments, socks.

VIII.

Sun has grayed the dock posts. June is still cold, sea-water wise. The boat's motor idles.

Precedence dictates that the world will reconfigure like fluid around their absence, and function on. Their absence will probably come sooner than mine. It is the way they would have it.

My calves are longer now when I dangle them over the edge of the float. My shoes triangulate.

After loading the sofa covered in plastic off of the dock into the back of her husband's lobster boat, we sit on the sofa, my head on her lap. She mopped my vomit off of the attic stairs when I was thirteen at 1 a.m.; her mother radar went off, she knew something was wrong, came out of her bedroom. My vision is slanted, edge of boat, edge of her bosom, soft body I never knew when pre-child thin and sinewy. Now we talk of different things, unintended pregnancies. Land development. No point in dwelling. I only knew her soft.

I would like to soothe the ache of that hole where lived old friends who died, who keep dying, the hole where you number among the last. I won't. Just as I'll not be consoled when you go, just as nothing will fill or be there to be filled. You call yourself old, I call myself worn. By future losses whose shape I cannot paint. I would like always to be a pair. Like blue jeans. I would like to paint your shape and hold it there, in sunlight.

September does what it always does, red and receding.

Their shapes flicker and glisten, gesturing. They gesture for my head to turn, turn forward, to look down at my hands, lucid.

A clothesline. A wide tree. A baby garden bed, darkened with water lugged from the well.

Simple to describe: Two soft-spoken people choose a different life, a life close only to each other. They go about things quietly, grace thundering behind them. Wisdom gentle, light-catching: glass, fish, water.

No one positioned to inherit their place. Simple. No one will live how they lived; no one will be who they were. Simple. The home will sleep. Simple. The light won't get up again.

Nairobi, Kenya

JACQUELINE
AND THE
NEGATIVE
IMAGINATION

Jacqueline was twenty-nine years old when I met her in 2013. She was the newest member of the Survival Girls, a women's theater group for Congolese refugees that I facilitated in a Nairobi slum in 2011. The group began as an arts workshop and within two weeks it had become a theater group whose first project was creating a piece to perform in public on World Refugee Day 2011. As their first piece of drama took shape, the women chose the theme of survival for how they would be known: The Survival Girls.

Over the years to follow, the Survival Girls has sustained itself as a self-governed theater group of these Congolese women, creating original theater based on social justice issues. The group grew as the women took on the roles of chairlady and treasurer, deepened their friendships, and received occasional contracts from humanitarian agencies in the refugee community in Nairobi to create original theater pieces about AIDS, gender-based violence, and the importance of education for girls.

When I returned to Nairobi in the summer of 2013, I met Jacqueline. Jacqueline's voice was deep, her body stout and she wore her hair back in a simple ponytail. It was her story the Survival Girls drew from most heavily that summer for their newest piece of original theater, which traced a refugee's journey from Congo (which the Survival Girls call "Congo" and not "The Democratic Republic of Congo") to Kenya.

The play begins in Congo, where a young woman and her mother are cooking at home. A rebel soldier, played by Jacqueline, raps on the door and barges in, ties up the daughter while he rapes her mother, then rapes the daughter. The soldier then leaves and the daughter cradles her mother, who dies in her arms. The daughter gathers her possessions and flees on foot. She boards a bus whose conductor kicks her off because she doesn't have the fare. A good Samaritan helps her to another bus station, and the driver of the next bus rapes her, telling her that sex is her payment for the fare. When she arrives in Kenya, a refugee agency sends her to a camp, where she is reunited with a family member. The Survival Girls join each other onstage for the finale, which is a song they sing in a mix of French and English: *Dire non à la violence/ We don't want to suffer anymore/ Dire non à la violence/ Non à la guerre...*

When the Survival Girls came up with the plot of this piece in our workshop, Jacqueline spoke a Congolese dialect of Swahili in her low voice while another Survival Girl translated for her. Jacqueline sat on the floor, leaning against the wall, wiping her eyes.

She told her own story, translating it from memory-image to language; it was translated for me by a member of the Survival Girls; and then the Survival Girls set to work translating the story for the stage. When it came time to cast the characters, Jacqueline agreed (and perhaps even volunteered; I'm not sure, because I have little Swahili) to play the men who did this to her, the men who raped her. The refugee women and

Kenyan counselors who eventually saw the production would comment on how perfectly Jacqueline embodied a rebel soldier's walk and talk and mannerisms.

This was not depicted in the play: Jacqueline saw her brother chopped up and the men who did it ordered her to make a stew with him. When she refused, they raped her, and she had a baby boy. She does not know if the baby boy survives.

In a profound way, there is no "telling" of this or any other part of Jacqueline's history—any kind of telling.

There is no speaking for her.

There is also no "telling" if it is true.

By "true" I mean "confirmed according to the rigors of journalistic standards." For Jaqueline, her story, and those of the lives of others in these pages who have undergone the unspeakable, the business of "confirming" the facts of history can be anything from futile and damaging, and for the purposes of humanitarian work, they can be entirely beside the point. Her story is deeply sourced in that it is hers, and that she told it, and that she is a wellspring.

Beyond a YouTube video made by a social service charity in which Jacqueline's face is blurred out for anonymity and her words are subtitled in English, there is no more direct record of Jacqueline telling it. And there is no Jacqueline here represented; she is *there*, vulnerable to violence and as yet unable to leave Kenya, awaiting asylum and living in poverty.

This writing is my attempt to ruminate about the theoretical implications of a severe trauma victim impersonating one's own rapist, as Jacqueline had the extraordinary bravery to do. The discerning will note that, while I explore a few theoretical claims about the effect of severe trauma on the psyche, this attempt lacks a central thesis. Such absence is meant to honor the unknowable in the violence spoken of here, the unknowability of the painful memories Jacqueline drew from to do what she did on that stage. It is meant as a gesture towards the possibility of the problematic notion of conducting scholarship as an ally. At the nexus of scholarship and spectacle, I do this work and this writing. None of it escapes the valid arguments of critique, but none of it would I undo.

There is no telling. That's why I tell it slant.

When I was in college, majoring not in international relations, development, or theater, but in literary arts, six years before I traveled to Kenya and met the women who would become the Survival Girls, I wrote this in my journal:

And were a man in rags or a man in a nice suit to turn aggressively towards me, to grab me, then and only then perhaps he would no longer be an image. Today a lecturer on Latin American torture testimony demonstrated this problem of discourse on pain: he took a piece of paper, meant to stand for discourse on torture, and ripped it. He said this is violence. This is what violence does. It is not discursive, it is violence, it is pain. No one will ever be there to see the swan on that water, or see me seeing it, in this particular weak winter light. Even I am not there anymore. I read that little Congolese girls are being impregnated by U.N. soldiers. You would tell me that becoming incapacitated by depression over it does nothing to help. You and your face and sweater, the talking with, the remembering of... came through the door, crowing about nuggets of wisdom and central philosophies and how he was right to say that a capacity for joy in one's own life can be a gift to other people, and he looked down at the buttons on his shirt. I walked out, and twice on my Crying Walk, a blue-eyed custodial worker stopped to smile at me and make sure I was smiling, and I felt guilty to be one of those pea-coated ear-phoned tortured youngsters. But he smiled and meant it, once on the street and once actually slowing the car, pointedly touching his cheeks, until I smiled.
(Other people with awful lives)

When Freud did his work on what he called the aetiology of hysteria in the late 1890s, connecting emotional disturbance in the women he treated with sexual assault that they had suffered in their past, he described those women as "suffering from reminiscences," which is perhaps the only phrase of his that I agree with and find productive in this discussion. The way I think of it is that trauma leaves marks that are invisible as well as visible.

It is those "invisible marks" that interest me as a scholar of performance, as a creative researcher, as the director of the Survival Girls' play, as a development worker, as a person. These marks could be said to create an "invisible freak" identity in a body whose limits and porousness are called into question by such intangible contagion as the memory-trace of trauma.

Trauma is inherent to the refugee experience—at the very least, that of the loss of one's home and an imminent sense of danger, and at most a chain of murder, rape, fleeing armed forces or people, losing all possessions, losing family, seeing them murdered, being tortured. Working with refugees is working with traumatized persons, and Nairobi's UNHCR office has processed well over 500,000 refugees. I believe that it is incumbent upon me, even as I find beauty and poetry in the "developing nations" I have gone to at will, to at all times consider the constraints that culture and my own vocabularies place on my examination of trauma—of anything—in people of different cultures than mine, especially those people who don't have the resources and privileges that I do.

Violence and its aftermath disrupt the very systems of the mind and body that structure and order experience; they erode those mechanisms by which a person does things that can be described as "conduct research." In these pages I can only cobble together the mosaic that might best honor such a conundrum under the murky title of "creative research," and ask questions that gesture towards the liminal—because ethical engagement with the suffering of others requires me, I believe, to honor the gaps.

If, as Rachel Adams contends in her reflections on Toni Morrison's novel *Beloved*, "identity… is rooted firmly in the physical body," then how does violation of the body impact the identity of the violated? We know appearance-based discrimination exists. What about experience-based discrimination? If the human body is a "figure through which culture is processed and oriented" (Halberstam and Livingston), is it also one through which violence is processed and oriented—or isn't processed, and is disoriented. Providing an arena in which to ask these questions, what is called in the academy a "creative-critical approach," allows a fruitful starting point for those seeking alternative and inclusive ways to conceptualize the traumatized condition.

In the anthology *Posthuman Bodies*, editors Judith M. Halberstam and Ira Livingston refer to nodes as loci where posthuman bodies "emerge:" "Where bodies, bodies of discourse, and discourses of bodies intersect to foreclose any easy distinction between actor and stage, between sender-receiver, channel, code, message, context."

Severe trauma sometimes results in what Western medicine defines as Schizophrenia, and sometimes in what it would define as Multiple Personality Disorder (or MPD; also known as Dissociative Identity Disorder, or DID). The academic theorist Allucquere Roseanne Stone discusses MPD in her essay in *Posthuman Bodies*. A summary of MPD/DID, as Stone elucidates it, might be that someone with the condition never has access to all her memories at once. Perhaps it's the brain's way of granting itself mercy; if you're not the person it happened to, then you don't remember it, and so one's subjectivity divides like a cell does, and for the same reason: to survive.

Yet this and any of my summaries falls short; Stone asserts that "the idea that personal identity is so refractory is a culturally specific one," reminding me to consider the constraints that my own culturally shaped subjectivity and vocabulary place on my examination of trauma in other cultures and bodies. In an essay about MPD/DID, Anthony Kubiak specifies that it is a rather recent and "distinctly American invention," pointing out that "what is often overlooked in both recovered memory and DID therapy, and in performance and performance theory, is the rather obvious intersection between certain modes of American religious practice, performance, and pathology." That cultural "disclaimer" given, MPD/DID is a point of interest because it could be described as a condition in which new boundaries crop up *within* the interiority of a human being, drawing borders between personalities, a divided subjectivity in which each personality functions as a different "node of agency."

The schizophrenic experience, in turn, is arguably one wherein "nodes of agency" are distributed *beyond* the boundaries of the body. "The schizophrenic," writes the philosopher Shaun Gallagher in his interdisciplinary work *How The Body Shapes The Mind*, "feels that he is not the agent of his own actions, and that he is under the influence of others—some persons or things seem to be moving his body." In other words, the schizophrenic's thoughts feel like they've come from without, often in the form of commands from certain objects or other "nodes of agency." Gallagher goes on to distinguish between ownership and agency, arguing that the loss of the latter is what characterizes some positive symptoms of schizophrènia, including that of "inserted thoughts:" "Action itself is experienced as owned, but the source of the action, an intention or command, is disowned." The feminist performance art scholar, Peggy Phelan, in her essay "Trisha Brown's *Orfeo*," describes Orfeo's experience as he leads his wife Eurydice out of the underworld, trying not to look back at her and thereby lose her forever, in terms that might be understood through Gallagher's lens of schizophrenia: "Orfeo begins to doubt…Orfeo hears a noise whose source he cannot place." Gallagher writes that "schizophrenic patients feel alienated not just from their own thought and action; they also feel alienated from affects, from their own body and skin, from their own saliva, from their own name, etc." Phelan pairs the experience of watching Brown's production of *Orfeo* with that of visiting the hospital bedside of her beloved Julie, whose brain tumor left her comatose, and whose fevered skin turning gray sends Phelan into "a space without geometry or physics, a space without subject or perceiver." Such liminal spaces are perhaps most faithful to the experience of the aggrieved, of the traumatized, of the realm of disturbance as it occurs and as it "happens to."

In her "Cyborg Manifesto," Donna Haraway, feminist scholar in science and technology, asks, "Why should our bodies end at the skin?" Why, indeed? The posthuman conversation is one that interrogates the boundaries of the body just as the postmodern conversation is one that interrogates boundaries, period. The bodies that are in this liminal landscape, whether that landscape is created by innate neurological wiring or by loss and trauma, could arguably all be posthuman ones.

I begin in the lexicon of criticism, wading through its boggy fields. Or I start where the poetry does, breathing in the mud around me. Either way, quicksand awaits. Bending forward without changing body: the converging streets do in the black pelt of midnight. By "midnight" the streets become prosaic. Anything worth reading is worth reading twice, including the text of another body, another person's history. If for every door in a fictional world there are nonfictional, discursive implications as to what is behind it, then it could be said that for every novel there should be a book of essays somewhere. The puppeteer who chooses the wallpaper of our internal bedrooms, the rooms we imagine (determine) separate fact from fiction, is a trickster, a coyote howling at a full moon—a full moon that prompts many a love sonnet only because it triggers certain biological reactions in certain warm-blooded vertebrates. (This is the way it is now: parameters soggy, weak.) Below the rung that determines (as a fact) that fact and fiction are false constructs, there is one that states that an equal mound of truth exists for every mound of untruth: we open doors into fictive pastimes for ourselves if we stop, while reading an essay, to do any kind of imagining. It is comforting, somehow: anytime something is fancied, there is something to be known; any time a reality feels too cold and hard there is a steaming mug of myth somewhere in the cosmos. Tricking our own brains into thinking we remember doing something we dreamed instead. So in a way I am from here, in that nothing but my own memory, the set of snapshots my brain calls fact, contests that I have not always been in a city on the East Coast at this deserted intersection near a convenience store, wondering at the sparkling bits in the sidewalk, waiting for another platonic shift.

While I believe all of them suffer to some degree from post-traumatic stress disorder and its attendant bouts of dissociation, anxiety and depression, and while their preparing for their performances prompts occasional flashbacks, none of the Survival Girls, that I know of, have been diagnosed as schizophrenic or as having multiple personalities. The flashbacks I do see, look from without like a blank facial expression, followed by sobs, and when they are with me, and I have asked permission to touch them, ensuing embraces and pressure-point touches to "bring them back" from the traumatic node that has robbed them of agency in the present moment. When they "come back," the Survival Girls often tell me:

"I can't control my thoughts. I can't stop replaying what happened. I'm afraid I'll never be like the other girls. I'm not a normal person. I can't stay where I am; I keep going back."

They also tell me they take strength from creating material drawn from memories of the violations they have suffered; they are the ones who asked to use the space of our workshop to create theater about those memories and who chose to continue the group when I flew back to America. There are vestiges of colonialism all over this work, and certainly they crop up any time I speak "on behalf of" or even about these women, especially to a privileged audience. I presume to do so because the marks left by trauma identify these women *to themselves* as carriers of dirtiness and shame: the worst kind of what feminist scholar and author of *Volatile Bodies: Toward a Corporeal Feminism* Elizabeth Grosz might term "outside-in inscription." That inscription might create a subjective space in the mind wherein the dirty, shaming thoughts that belonged to others begin to feel like our own when they did not originate within us. "Self-identity," write Halberstam and Livingston, "is ultimately a system of parasitic invasion, the expression within me of forces originating from the outside."

When the Survival Girls have unkind thoughts about themselves, where do those thoughts come from?

The assumptions and problems with this question, and with the work I do that engages it, resound, as do other questions about my work with the Survival Girls that I have as a scholar: to borrow from Rachel Adams' description of the term "queer," is the identity of a rape victim "a concept that refuses the logic of identity politics, and the irreconcilable problems of inclusion and exclusion that necessarily accompany identitarian categories?"

Rare is the cultural space wherein admission of her status as a rape victim will not garner a woman derision; perhaps nonexistent is the person whose identity did not originate from the outside as a cultural creation. The effect of such "inner-outer confusion" as that produced by subjectively-reinforced stigma might a body that is "deviant," to use Rachel Adams' term, in ways we can't see: a raped woman, an "invisible freak" who believes she is dirtied by an aspect of her experience in which

108

she didn't have a choice, but who does have a choice in its reenactment.

It is possible that the self-hating feelings described to me by the Survival Girls are a living testament to the notion that a person's status as "freak" need not be visible. It is possible that some forms of deviance derive from remembered experience and are not always embodied visually—but that when they are, they look like Jacqueline as a soldier, bellowing onstage. The notion of "nodes" may extend to this discussion of the experience of violence and the repression of its memory. Dissociation, a common and involuntary response of the nervous system of an overpowered body to abuse (and perhaps what the Survival Girls were describing when they told me of their inner plight), might be described this way: the raped and/or post-raped body has a "node" up in the far corner of the room, a "safe" vantage point wherefrom the witness watches her own body used like a rag doll, a necessary and involuntary division of self in a moment of crisis. (Phelan, again: "a space without subject or perceiver.") And yet, violence may offer the discussion of posthuman bodies their one indissoluble boundary, the one scenario in which the distribution of agency and therefore of *responsibility* cannot take place beyond the boundaries of one's skin. In a rape, between a rapist and a victim, there are two distinct bodies; to tell the victim there are not, strikes me as unthinkable. If the post-traumatic or schizophrenic body is one I can grasp calling posthuman in that its borders may not "end at the skin," the real-time raped body is not.

Perhaps the "nodes" that do make sense in this discussion would be that in-the-moment dissociation from violence and the self-contained memory of that violence that intrudes suddenly in traumatic flashback. "Memory as it attaches itself to unresolved trauma," writes Anthony Kubiak, "is intolerable not because it has been 'repressed,' but rather because it will not be translated." He quotes Cathy Caruth's introduction to *Trauma: Explorations in Memory,* "What returns in flashback is not simply an overwhelming experience that has been obstructed by a later repression or amnesia, but an event that is itself constituted, in part, by its lack of integration into consciousness."

Here the node of traumatic memory itself, a memory that precludes smooth "translation" of self from past to present, is often buried for the sake of that continuation-of-self except in uncontrollable moments of flashback. And in those moments, the node of agency running the show is that of traumatic memory, loosened to wreak havoc on the subjectivity of the survivor.

Gallagher posits that a "lack" of "protension" (a "motor process that precede[s] action and translate[s] intention into movement") is responsible for the loss of *agency*, but not *ownership*, of the schizophrenic's thoughts and actions, because "without protension, in cases of both intended thought and of unintended thinking, thinking will occur within the stream of consciousness that is not experienced in the making." In other words, thinking "occur[ing] within the stream of consciousness that is not experienced in the making" could be thinking that "will not be translated," that will not be "integrat[ed] into consciousness." Such unintegrated thinking is a powerful node, one capable of robbing the self inside a raped or traumatized body of agency, one capable of convincing that self that she is dirty, that she deserves what she got, that she'll never be normal, that she should be ashamed.

> *Somewhere my face assumes its less affordable set of features under a shapeless grey hood. It is what I do in gas stations in strange towns. It is what I do at night. The damage is not something I ask for, but I do imagine it, and I am superstitious. I am trying to enter it, but it is a wall, and shifts like tiles.*
>
> *One: there is a scar on my ear where damage has been done. In an intimate moment you kiss it and I weep. My first laugh, after months, tears at the air with the silver strength of departure.*
>
> *The latch is missing.*
>
> *Two: there is a white fog surrounding us on a beach and I tell you that you can feel and look at the pink and ridged place where they have lopped my thumb off. You break into tears and my own sob sounds like a bark and I say, this is what it is. If it's here, it is. The stones around us are flat and autumn-colored.*

The Survival Girls rehearsed in Nairobi's Kangemi neighborhood, in the studio-sized apartment of the most senior Survival Girl, Sofia, moving her plastic chairs to the far side of the room and using the kitchen as backstage. Jacqueline would come in from outside the tiny apartment, where laundry hung over puddles of sewage and wandering feral dogs, clomping her big boots and carrying a "gun," a large piece of wood she carried over her shoulder. The Survival Girls had kept some red sashes from costumes for another piece of theirs (the red sashes had symbolized the blood of war), and one of those red strips of cloth was now repurposed as Jacqueline's "gun" strap. The Survival Girls determined that for the performance of this piece, which would be at a local Non-Governmental Organization (NGO) for refugee women called Heshima Kenya, Jacqueline's soldier character would drag the victims offstage for the rape scene, and the victims would scream to illustrate what was happening to them.

In a February 2005 TED Talk, Anna Deveare Smith, acclaimed performer of one-woman shows that she compiles faithfully from interview transcripts, performs four monologues. One of them is based on the story told to her by a female prison inmate about how she allowed her boyfriend to abuse and kill her daughter. Smith prefaces the piece by saying people had asked her to take it out, because the character was not likable. She demurred, she tells her audience, because she values risk and "the negative imagination."

What is the negative imagination? What is the process by which one "plays the bad guy," the way Jacqueline and Smith both did? What does that process do and make possible for a performer who, like Jacqueline, suffered at the hands of the bad guy she's playing? Author Anne Anlin Cheng writes in her book, *The Melancholy of Race: Psychoanalysis, Assimilation, and Hidden Grief* of Smith's work:

> Anyone who has partaken of Smith's performances understands the discomfort of being made to watch the fine line between speaking for, speaking as, and speaking against… With Smith's peculiar brand of impersonation, it is as if only in imitation, in the bodily occupation of the other, that we come to see paradoxically an alternative to the traps of representation. That is, representation has frequently and rightly been criticized

for its colonizing potentials. But Smith's art suggests that representation, mimicry even, may be employed as a form of performative counteroccupation, whereby the act of placing oneself in the other's place exposes one's vulnerability to that performed other.

A language barrier, and also a desire not to further invade or trouble Jacqueline's process of recovery and ownership, prevented me from asking her in-depth what it meant for her to portray her rapist. I wondered where her "self" went in the moments when she used her body to perform a "counteroccupation," to tell the story of the person who so assaulted her selfhood (or so it seemed to me as a "viewer" of her story). Did that "counteroccupation expose [her] vulnerability to that performed other," or did it *reduce* that vulnerability by producing a space of assertion, a node of agency in the body of Jacqueline herself, in order for her to perform that counteroccupation?

From their very first improvisation of the first rape scene, the Survival Girls had it down so well that I could barely breathe watching it. I am affected by every rehearsal of every piece the Survival Girls create, but with this one I could barely hold the camera to record them. Jacqueline was awe-inspiring, and so was Palome, re-enacting her own rape at the hands of rebel soldiers with high, keening screams. They tied some of their red sashes together to make a large red "rope" that the Survival Girls, who played truck drivers, carried around themselves, making engine noises as they held it out at elbow level on either side, to denote a car. The red rope behind the "driver" would drag on the ground until Patience's refugee character "boarded" by slipping within its circle and holding up the slack, not unlike how a maid of honor would hold a wedding dress train. Two more sashes were used by Jacqueline in that very first scene, when she tied up Palome's soon-to-be-refugee character and dragged Sofia's mother character backstage as Sofia wailed and Palome screamed.

When we are talking about bodies that have been raped, and that re-enact that rape as the perpetrator, what kind of translation is that? Are we talking about metaphor? When it is physically *represented* instead of physically undergone, "translated" from choiceless victimization to voluntary representation, does it become metaphor?

No, if we touch it is through space. Boundless space, you call it, but you are lying. The space you are in must have bounds, because it isn't here. If that space were truly boundless, this space would be too. It would all be one space, and we would be in it together.

Apparently the first thing to do to avoid an attack is not to look like a victim. Be alert. Look around. Be aware. On the grass we startle passersby with our loud, throat-tearing shouts of "no!" as would-be attackers simulate threatening postures and words. We throw out our hands, our feet. We back up, turn and run.

When I was young I saw everyone else's bodies but since I was inside my own I more existed. I didn't think I transcended what I saw moving about, I just... was. I wonder now if this is the closest I will get to remembering the brain state of my infancy: my body wasn't set yet, its perimeters as the same as those binding up everyone else weren't apparent to me. I didn't relate what went on in my head with the fact that somewhere my foot ended and something else began.

As the Survival Girls developed their piece, I arranged for them to perform at Heshima Kenya, an organization assisting refugee girls with holistic approaches to trauma recovery and reintegration into society. Earlier in the week of the performance, I traveled there to make clear to the counselors the risk of triggering traumatic memories in the audience members. I knew it helped the Survival Girls themselves to express what had happened onstage, and also, I hoped that if we took proper care of audience members who reacted to the piece, the Survival Girls could help them as well.

"The ones who react, we will know to give them counseling," said Alice, the Heshima counselor I spoke with. "It's why Heshima is here."

The day came, and the Survival Girls did their piece justice. After their performance, they bowed and went "backstage" (which meant "into the kitchen"), and Alice had all fifty young women in the audience (Burundian,

Somali, Rwandan, Congolese, Ethiopian) close their eyes and take five deep breaths. They had begun the play noisily giggling at Jacqueline's spot-on impression of a man, but by the end of the play, you could have heard a pin drop. In the silence that followed those five breaths, the howling began. Full-on screams in two cases; girls running outside and lying on the grass, pounding with their fists, while counselors rubbed their backs. I slipped backstage, where the girls, who could hear the cries, were all tearing up also. Jacqueline burst into loud sobs and wept against the back wall for a while. I put a hand on her shoulder, and told her I was proud of her. ("Her suffering," writes Phelan of her beloved dying Julie, "or what I took to be her suffering, was sometimes too much for me to watch... There was little I could do... mainly I stood next to her.")

I walked with Jacqueline back to huddle with the other girls, sniffling, and I told them to listen to the cries emanating from the other room. "Each of those girls will get help now," I said, "because you were brave enough to do this today."

One of the counselors came back to ask if I'd do group therapy with the audience. "They're *all* crying," she said, concerned and perplexed. "Would you do group therapy?"

So the Survival Girls and I, none of us with counseling degrees, thereby risked the well-being of the girls in the audience by attempting to counsel them in anyway. First we did our customary end-prayer huddle in our little group, then we came outside and sat in a big circle. Fifty girls, some hiding behind their headscarves. I thought we should be in smaller groups, and after a few awkward silences in the face of questions put forth by the counselors, we branched off and every Survival Girl and I sat with a group of about eight audience members. The Survival Girls took on the role of counselor unexpectedly, but they did very well. Truth be told, most of the audience members didn't know why anyone would want to relive or think about those memories. They wanted tangible ("embodied," perhaps) help; they wanted to move forward, the way Jacqueline just wants to see some practical benefit of her work in the Survival Girls. "If people support us," she reasoned once in Swahili as Sofia translated for me, "then why aren't we seeing the profit?" None of the Survival Girls or their audience members wanted to stew for the sake of stewing. All of them want to go to school, and most of them are college-age, which is how old I was the first time I attempted to write about violence happening to other bodies.

Poetry is what is done in the quietness of study, in response to the loudest sounds, what happens when a disempowered, gaunt little ghost of a child—cannot stop thinking of the row of cottonwoods lining the dirt driveway to her family's barn; specifically, the grey of their bark, specifically, the artichoke plant between each of them, which leads to the mother in the garden and the strange smell of the little garden shed and so on. The noise made by phenomena that remain silent until allowed by the (loose-fitting, and cursed with the affective/effective nature of the observer's affect/effect on the observed) media of memory, then language, then pen, to bloom out or pool, or do what it is that wounds do in their language in order to have a language. It is a response to the gaping pink, stretching sort of noise wounds make. First the noise (tear?), then the quiet in which words are worked with. It's merely a reproduction of the only script there is: all matter, once localized, bursting forth with a fury beyond fury—think of a rose, its petals piercing you—the soft womb of silence in which the planets have since bloomed out and glided into their velvet orbits, sweeping through the vacuum of space like owls...

The sounds of the Survival Girls' screams in rehearsal and onstage replay in my mind when I read the words of, for instance, Paula Rabinowitz, the author of *They Must Be Represented: The Politics of Documentary*, in which she quotes documentary filmmaker Chick Strand about American porn: "It's not that they take responsibility for the experience happening but for 'having had' it. The claim of 'responsibility' challenges women's victimization in/by narrative by asserting that their stories are conscious reenactments." While I do not believe the circumstances referenced in Rabinowitz's piece translate perfectly to the experience of the Survival Girls, I do wonder if the Survival Girls' work "challenges women's victimization in/by narrative by asserting that their stories are conscious reenactments." As Jacqueline bellowed and wrestled her costars onto the stage floor, brandishing a piece of wood meant to symbolize a gun, did she feel fully present as herself, or was there a division of self, one produced by a collision of her personal memory of being a rape victim with the embodiment of her rapist? Adams writes of "the extraordinary body" as one that "becomes a signifier for the author's secret self." I wonder if the shame left by traumatic memories could be argued to constitute the raped person's "secret self:" was Jacqueline performing her "secret self" when she performed not her own body being violated again, but the affect and persona of her rapist, raping others? In Phelan's essay on Orfeo she writes, "His vertical mastery of the visible world is purchased through her collapse back into the underworld," but in my mind "he" is not Orfeo and "she" is not Eurydice: through his resurrection onstage, it's Jacqueline's *rapist* that "purchases his mastery of the visual world" through *Jacqueline's* "collapse back into the underworld," to wherever she goes when she plays him, to a place where trauma sometimes leaves no visible—"visual"—mark. I wonder if, in playing a man like the one who raped her, Jacqueline's experience overlapped with that which Phelan described as she recalled (in this same essay?) sitting at her beloved's bedside: "I felt a strange loosening, not a simple 'letting go,' a much more intense *turning from myself*. It was at once both painful and consoling, a kind of dream and a kind of horrible tearing" (emphasis mine).

That Jacqueline wanted to write the play and perform in the production as the soldier was clear. What it asked of her was not. Yet her tears when the play was over, as she stood against a wall, sobbing, suggest what Phelan reminds us of: that "this place of play insists that play is not easy."

As a child I had a picture book with exquisite illustrations called The Twelve Dancing Princesses. The princesses went every night to an enchanted castle where they danced their dancing slippers to tatters, but to get there and back they had to walk through a forest of silver, a forest of gold, and a forest of crystal. When it rains at night, drops clinging to dark branches lit from behind, hanging

like jewels, I am given a gift, I walk through my own conscious
wonderland. I see the bark glisten in the dark. Lately, I have been
ashamed. I have fallen back. The daydreams behind my irises but
in front of my brain (though I know, I know, they are inside it)
are clouding my vision; I cannot see as easily what is divine and
dripping with clusters of crystals. I am grasping in the dark. I am
walking to a saddening soundtrack, it is night too often, it is wet
too often, the sidewalks are dark with moisture too often, and I like
the sweet syrup of sadness too much. I am nursing its warmth, it
bleeds all over my face and into my eye sockets, I am blinded by
my own demonic devices to the miracle of my small square of light
in the quilt. Remember, I tell myself, barely tethered to my own
body, to the wet sidewalk, what you see is light, all we are is light
slowed down, and you don't even see much; we talk about miracles
as angels on the head of the pin, but have we talked about whether
we can see them, waltzing and iridescent?

If posthumanism is understood as the application of postmodern theoretical frameworks to critical discussions of the body, then it could be described as the admission that certain physical binaries are dissolvable. It might support the idea that Western claims to and of order with regard to bodies are interrogable: that we, inside bodies, don't really know what's going on, and that the world changes us and our bodies as much as we change it... that is, if a distinction between our bodies and the world exists. (Posthumanism might posit that it doesn't.) The traumatized condition is an experience that might be termed the "postmodern" experience of a "posthuman" body whose sense of agency and time, as well its physical borders, are malleable and porous. Beyond that I find no conclusion to draw about Jacqueline's extraordinary metamorphosis, because I fundamentally believe that there is no thesis statement for rape. Those other people with awful lives, which may at times and from some perspectives include the Survival Girls: they're why I tell it slant. Jacqueline has little to no shelter. It is not discursive it is violence it is pain.

That is why I ask more questions, and proffer fewer answers than is perhaps palatable from the perspective of nonfiction writing that purports to have any kind of critical bent. When a question mark announces itself, two things happen: one, more space blooms out, space implied by the impending search for answers. Two, that space is made discomfiting, uncomfortable, uneasy; things aren't clear and tidy, the way they would be if there were tidy answers to the question: *Why did Jacqueline want to (re) enact the soldier who raped her? What was that for her; what did it do?* If there are cogent ways to theorize about the interiorities of the humans rendered disordered misfits by profound trauma and unspeakable violence, I do not presume to know them. If there is a structure to violence, I do not presume to know it. I wonder if anyone but its victims can, or its perpetrators. The youngest Survival Girl's father was so traumatized by his detention and torture at the hands of rebel soldiers that he did not know how long he was detained or how many times. He did not, for years, know his own name.

A UNHCR worker told me that some refugee trauma victims in Nairobi live chained to the bed, their paranoia has become so deep. During a homestay in Ecuador in high school, I learned that my host mother was the executive director of the family planning organization. She had spent forty years dealing directly with the fallout and threat women in Ecuador experienced of sexual violence, and she brought me to work every day so I could see how things were. She was a devout Catholic. When I asked her if she believed in hell, she said simply, "*El infierno está aquí.*"

Hell is here, on this earth.

The Bible is where it's a symbol.

Another way of saying that might be that textual space is a metaphor for the horrors of lived violence.

And the theatrical space, for Jacqueline, could be that also.

The shifting is supposed to be the function of my brain. I have held myself up with the walls before, under the water.

I was participating in a kind of sexual voyeurism when my family got cable and I watched one of those soft porn shows on Starz in the wee hours after everyone had gone to bed. I was ten. I watched a B-movie with explicit sex in it and felt an achy heartbeat, only in the wrong place.

   Imagining the simultaneous funerals of all immediate family members is probably not normal. Winters whose ascension carries a freeze, give way like seduced bodies, supply, to sweet breeze. Lampposts, and by the mere imagining of it I realize that the people from whose forms mine is made tether me to this earth. Left to my own devices, I leave it in all but body. Leave it until the thought of violence leaves me conscious of the ways I am cradled by this night street, walking where I will. I think that the words "to humble" and "to ground" are similes is not an accident. I get to dream because I am safe. They hurt me, yes, but without tethers (velvet ropes) I think I might just run over the rim and fall upwards. Branches of a tree, if you're looking up from under the tree, are like veins of a leaf.

I was at the border crossing between Syria and Turkey earlier in the summer on my way into the Atmeh refugee camp in Syria, weeks before the 2013 chemical attack in Damascus.

   I was there for the same reason that brought me to Nairobi—refugee advocacy—and while I toured the refugee camp just within Syria without incident, violence has since transpired there. On that day violence touched all of us standing in the sun by the olive trees through its memory, and if not that, through its possibility. But what web am I describing, of the tension in the air comprised of possible violence? If it didn't belong to me, in that it neither happened to me nor did I bear a memory of it, then in my attempt to describe it I am giving words to the kind of violence that robs its victims of the ability to use words. I would be theorizing the unspeakable, and able to do so because it doesn't belong to me, not unlike a person who visited the World Trade Center as a tourist on September 10th, 2001. It does lead to questions of human bodies' movement through time and space. Certainly the argument that the two are illusions, that the human mind invents them, that they're malleable, feels far away if one is in the place where children are gunned down and disemboweled, where schools are bombed. But that's not where I was. I was in the place, but not at the time.

That which is visible in the world around us abounds, and of it we only see slivers. What we register visually is shaven down to what we know, which is to say, shaven down by gigantic leaps and bounds. We see what we know to be there, hemmed down by what we don't want to admit is there, slimmed down by what we have time for, blurred down yet even more by the fact that most of the time, we are not actively seeing objects in front of us; rather, we are daydreaming, and looking at the movie behind our irises. I am writing and the shadows of my fingers intersect; as I write each respective light source casts a different shadow. My pen tip's shadows fall at four different points on the paper at varying levels of intensity. There are four different light sources in the room. Depending on the areas where more shadows prevent light from reaching the page directly, some parts of the myriad soft curved—but even in dissecting this I haven't conveyed what I meant to; what I mean is, the shadows of my fingers are like a sea animal, like some other fold in the body, like fallopian tubes, like soft sea grasses. The shadows of my fingers betray their bodiness, their sameness to all those other folds and biologically alive shapes, more than the fingers themselves. Fingers lose their fingerness. On the page a nest of soft line and curve I can't hope to replicate.

A body
Fold is a body
Fold.

When I worked with the Survival Girls, I changed buses in Nairobi, which required being downtown in a grittier city part than lush Westgate (the mall where I would type up these notes about the Survival Girls, that was attacked by Al-Shabaab two days after I left Nairobi in a two-day hostage crisis). However, there was a Hilton gym there in the city center, and I would go through the metal detectors, hand uniformed guards my backpack, and go up to where the pine smell of the sauna room would lull me into my remix of the Emotional Freedom Technique: touch pressure points, and all the while recite the things that bring me back into the present (though what "me" and "the present" are, exactly, remains debatable). "My name is Ming. I'm twenty-eight." Tap the temples. "I'm in Nairobi." Tap the cheeks and above the lips. "I have a place I can come and relax that I am grateful for." Touch the tips of the fingers with the other tips, and tap them together. "Today I worked with women who amaze me and whom I love, and they don't have these things, and I'm sad about that. It's September seventeenth, twenty thirteen..." And so on. Twice I got a massage from women who told me how they pray. One of them had lost two sons. There was tea outside the massage room. Chamomile.

I think of the eyes of the men I saw at the checkpoint, some in military vests, holding guns near the crowds of children. I think of Jacqueline holding her fake gun, Jacqueline sobbing by the wall, Jacqueline bellowing over the bodies of her fellow players. Jacqueline going back to her scant bed in the slums while I got my massage at a hotel in the city. We never had a conversation that wasn't mediated, and she doesn't grace these pages. Not the woman in Nairobi. It's only the memory trace of her, permuted over and over again through a kaleidoscope of refractions and contrivances, through the process of recalling and writing about an act of catharsis and courage I can barely describe, let alone understand. Through my attempt to comprehend, the woman who is the referent, the woman violated, has again been violated here.

Jacqueline.

[Jacqueline.]

[   ]

Drummondville, Quebec

THANK YOU
FOR YOUR
ADVICES

At 6 a.m. Dianne showers. We went to bed three hours ago, but my flight is in three hours, and I have a train to catch. When she comes in she is squinting a little. "I'm just around," she says sleepily. Neither of us are naturally early risers. The winter dawn outside is lovely in a cold and quiet way. I haven't been up to see it since getting to Drummondville three days ago. Dianne hasn't been up to see it since getting to Drummondville seven weeks ago.

*

In the Montreal Airport the US Customs guy looks at me. He says I've been picked for a random bag check.

He picks up my green pack of American Spirits.

He sees my eyes widen.

"Are they illegal to take?" I ask.

He shakes his head.

"You look tired," he says. "Are you tired?"

Dianne has a tablet. She got it in Nairobi for cheap. It is an iPad. We joke about how obviously it was stolen. Dianne says she didn't use it for a month after buying it because she was scared she might somehow be found and thought to be the thief.

On my first day with her, three older guests come. They are members of what Dianne calls the "Congolese Welcome Committee." It's unclear how official the committee is. I retreat to Dianne's bedroom and try to understand a letter from my boss. I was supposed to teach acting for him. He added me as a friend on Facebook and said he thought the recent bombing in Paris was like their 9/11 and so I thought his sharing of personal political beliefs meant it was okay to tell him I felt nervous. I feel nervous before doing any new thing. Now he wants to change my contract and not pay me for spending hours "shadowing" someone else because I told him I felt nervous and he has decided that means I'm not ready.

Dianne guts a fish. I stand behind her and put my chin on her shoulder.

I ask what I can do.

"Observe," she says.

*

"Yes," I say. "Just out from Drummondville."

"What were you doing *there?*"

"Visiting a friend."

*

"Is there anything you'd like to do that is easier to do with someone else?" I ask her. "Anything new you'd like to try, or a new place you'd like to go?"

"I want to go where the people are like this," she says, moving her arms smoothly and laterally across the ground.

"Where they... skate? You mean ice skating?"

*

"How do you have a friend in Drummondville?"

"She was a refugee. I met her in Kenya."

*

First there is the question of where there is a rink. "Rink?" Place to skate. "Oh, there is one just there." She points.

Two blocks from the house she shares with her older brother, who is quiet with his scripture, and her nephew, who is quiet with his journal.

How could I be surprised that there is a rink so close? This is Quebec, Canada. It's free. But there aren't places to rent skates.

"There is a secondhand shop just there." She points again.

And so there is. But are there skates? She asks in French of the lady who points us downstairs. Are there ever skates! We find ones to fit me that are new, and ones to fit her that we rob laces off another one to complete. We keep laughing and falling into the musty old coats.

Dianne and I like to laugh together, at home and in the thrift store trying on skates and in the supermarket debating the merits of hard lemonade.

*

"How do you have a friend in Drummondville?"

"She was a refugee. I met her in Kenya."

I realize as he holds an empty bottle for headache tincture I bought at my yoga studio that she is still a Congolese refugee. I hold my tongue, though. It wouldn't do to ramble. Not least because the tincture is of poppy, and perhaps illegal.

*

There is a group of people standing when we arrive at the rink with our skates in the red bags. There is someone lying on their back holding their head. A bystander tells Dianne in French what happened, and all I understand is his multiple eye rolls. Dianne translates: there was a woman who fell and her eyes keep rolling back. The ambulance will come. They are waiting on the car from the hospital. Then the young boys will be allowed back into the rink. Everyone will be allowed back in.

125

A stretcher is brought onto the ice. In my memory, which is days old, both the woman's jacket and the ambulance are black and green.

*

We skate. She points first to what look like pieces of a black jungle gym. They are for leaning on, for taking around on the ice like walkers.

I feel nervous about skating. So does Dianne. I'm from California and she's from Congo. We're equally in need of the walkers.

I worry for a moment that we will disrupt the swift kids. They skate circles around us. One other person is using the black walkers. A little girl. Her mother glides by us and her hair is long and dark and her smile bright. I tell her it's our first time. She takes a picture of Dianne and me. We put our walkers off to the side and hold hands to stand up so we won't look like newbies in the photo, which Jolie is excited to post because then her friends can see she is doing a cold-weather thing in her new cold-weather home. The lady has a son also, a teenager.

Dianne's nephew is a teenager. On my first day, in the late afternoon, he is writing at the table. In his journal. He's just writing for himself.

*

We whoop with laughter a lot. We did in Africa. We do here. I suspect it comes across differently. Like Dianne and the other Survival Girls, I can sometimes lift people's moods with my laughter and good cheer. Unlike Dianne and the other Survival Girls, it's unlikely that I would get kicked off a train in America for Laughing While Black. When Jennifer Lawrence flipped off the press corps after winning her Academy Award, she was found to be just that: winning. Were a girl who looked like Dianne to do that—in spite of the fact that Dianne is also beautiful and a talented actor— she would probably be labeled as sassy or rude. Sass is not "charming" on black girls the way it is on white ones.

Dianne is the least sassy person I know, most of the time. Her recommendation letter from the person at the refugee agency who directed the movie she starred in—a letter Dianne has saved in a laminated folder— says she is "unassuming but very talented," which sums it up nicely.

*

The customs guy opens my bag. A little yellow bag, a mini-mini-mini sort of duffel. The bag is yellow and of a South American print. I probably got it in Bolivia. I may also have gotten the little woven pouch he is holding up now in Bolivia. The one little pill he finds at the bottom turns out to belong to the bottle I take in case of the anxiety attacks that loomed up into my life five years ago. He seems disappointed when I show him the bottle, when the pill matches the others, and when the name on the bottle is the one on my passport.

*

Lupita Nyong'o comes up fairly quickly. My first morning in town Dianne enters from the living room, where she is sleeping on her other mattress so I can have her room, and she stands in her bright lace underwear from Nairobi and puts lotion on her face and legs. The lotion is in a label-less Tupperware container. I ask about it. She mixes it herself. The Nivea lotion by itself was giving her spots, so she mixed it with a product she brought from Nairobi, a gel that is antibacterial. Then the lotion didn't irritate her skin. Her skin is, from my perspective, flawless. I tell her so and she asks if I've seen the latest picture of Lupita Nyong'o. "She was in a dress," says Dianne, rubbing her skin, "and she was shining."

Dianne shows me another product that is to make sure her skin isn't too bright. I'm a little confused about the difference between bright skin and shining skin, and about the part of her beauty regimen that has to do with making sure her knuckles aren't darker than the skin of her hands. I am a white, thirty-one year old; my skin is freckled, medium pimpled, and now also wrinkled. Dianne is twenty-four and her skin is none of those things.

*

I also have one black leather bag from Nine West stuffed to the gills. My cousin gave it to me. I use it for its many pockets.

*

We walk in the rain to the market that has foreign foods because occasionally there is palm oil there. It is the strange kind of almost-dark of an afternoon covered in rain clouds. We walk arm-in-arm. There is rain in our hair. We blink in the rain at the crosswalk, and laugh that Dianne is not used to how people wait obediently at them.

There are aspects to the work I have done with Dianne and the girls, and my writing about that work, that I want to ask Dianne about. The worst criticism was probably doled out by someone I barely knew over Facebook, who typed to me: "You're using refugees to further your career, and it turns my stomach." This person and I had spoken maybe twice in our lives. She leveled her claims over Facebook messenger about a piece I wrote online two years earlier after going into a refugee camp in Syria. She'd clearly been waiting for two years for the chance to say what she felt about that article.

"Is there a way you'd like me to improve how I do my work?" I'd asked her.

"This isn't a customer service survey," she'd fired back.

"Oh *balls*," said my mother, making a wiping-away motion with her hand, when I repeated that line to her in California. As in, that's when you block the person who is not interested in constructive dialogue but who is interested in policing and bullying and trolling you.

At the time, though, I let the troll keep ranting on and on, until the cold I had kept at bay all that afternoon as I'd been interviewing a Syrian refugee claimed my head entirely.

The troll made sure to tell me she'd talked to other people at our masters program about this and they'd agreed with her.

That didn't pack the punch she hoped it would. I don't know what Dianne's bullying looked like, at her school in Nairobi, other than that it was about the memories she came from. Mine looked like some guy shouting, "What the fuck are you *talking* about?" in the middle of my comments in workshop. Or the same guy a year later, writing a "critique" of my story so vitriolic, nasty, and personal that he emailed of his own volition an hour or two later, apologizing for it. Or finding a classmate's public tweet naming me, and saying that I was a "fucking nutbag" and that she'd "never spend any money on anything [I] miraculously published."

Or an editor of the *Review* taking my hand in a coffee shop and saying he wanted to be someone I trusted, and to tell him about what had given me the post-traumatic stress, and then telling me a week later he'd changed his mind. I met with him and his managing editor to point out that they were about to reprint a translation that had seen print elsewhere, and showed them the proof. I also said I thought asking someone to share what had happened to them and then rescinding that was an awful way to treat them. The editor wouldn't let me finish, leaned toward me across the table, spread his arms. "Can we be done with this now?" he'd snapped. "Can we be friends?"

I asked if maybe they wanted to ask the Comparative Literature PhDs to weigh in on the translations to make sure they were good ones, since bad translations could incite a lot of ire with editors, and also, the comp lit PhD's are great people and love literature and might be a great addition to a poetry reading meeting. The editors exchanged looks, looked back at me, and said that "the review was too traditional" to institute a new change like that. Then they went back to updating the blog for the *Review*.

After breaking up with a girl in the program after less than six months of dating her, I was not ultimately surprised that she spent the following summer becoming very close with the people I'd introduced her to in that little Midwestern town while I was gone working in Bolivia. The reasons I'd broken it off with her had to do with signs of controlling and obsessive behavior, so it follows that when I returned from working abroad for my last year and it became clear to her that we were never ever ever getting back together, every piece of information I'd given her about my private life and family history circulated, often with certain embellishments. I gave her a no-contact request; she came to my door, left voicemails I didn't listen to, texted and emailed daily, and I got out of seminar to reports of her looking for me where she knew I had class. I started feeling frightened, and I had trouble sleeping well. I filed a restraining order, but some classmates were furious at me for doing so, so I rescinded it. She wrote long and detailed letters to my mother, citing Wikipedia articles about my antidepressants' side effects of "paranoia" and using the fact that I had sobbed on my bed once about how mean my classmates were as proof that I was paranoid. She even sent my mother a follow-up note to "correct typos" in the first. She claimed to be distraught and asking for empathy all over that little town, in every cafe, at every party, at professors' office hours, and it took some people a while to realize what was going on. Some of them never did.

The refugee-work troll, then, wasn't doing anything out of the ordinary for that place. It wasn't her opinion I was worried about. It was Dianne's. If the refugees themselves whom I had been working with for eight years in four different countries felt the way the troll did about my work for and with them, I would want to do what I could to fix it.

*

"You seem nervous. Are you nervous?" he asks.

"I've never done this before," I say.

"This is customs," he says, as though it wasn't obvious.

*

This is all to say that when I ask Dianne what her earliest memory was of Congo, sitting in her kitchen in Canada, six weeks after her first-ever plane ride took her over the Atlantic to Canada, and it is not carnage Dianne recalls but the bullying she faced in school before then, I understand why her face falls. I nod, and say I am sorry, and that I believe it is part of what makes her wonderful now. She says, "people who had not experienced that kind of unkind probably do not have the same awareness." I agree that it has deepened her, and that painlessness is another word for an unexamined life, which itself is probably another phrase for unconsidered actions. "You care about how you treat people now, Dianne," I said. "You are so good at dealing with them that I am asking your advice all the time."

*

We go on a cloudy walk across the downtown area. We find a wee art museum that is free and open to the public. Or: I look for one on Google maps for us to go explore. It is very quiet. There is an oil painting, one of those paintings that make use of the ridges and layers of paint to create a certain mood. Like Monet's lilies. Only this one is heavy on the reds and browns, and Dianne reaches out and touches it. Several feelings slam at once in me.

130

I should not have suggested this. I should make sure the docent doesn't see. I should explain how uptight *mzungus* are about this kind of thing. I should apologize for not telling her sooner. It had not occurred to me that she might touch it, and for this I feel especially sorry. I should chat with the docent about Dianne and about what it's like for refugees. No, all of those things are somehow problematic. So is writing into this piece that moment. It creates a piece of textual space wherein a white woman is writing about a black woman doing something locals in her new city might see as "unlearned." Maybe *I* am unlearned. So is the docent. Those paintings are infinitely touchable. It's their tactile nature that makes them so magnetic. And in any case, it's not my words that would ever solve this quandary. It's hers. Dianne's. Her words.

*

I've traveled to somewhere between twenty and thirty countries and worked in twelve of them. I have never before been selected for a random bag check.

*

On our last night we stay up late drinking wine. Her nephew joins us. He asks why I can't stay longer. I am overjoyed. This is the first thing he has said to me. I realize that all along he was glad I was there. As we are finishing the third bottle of wine he opens a prescription bottle. I become nervous for him. Dianne touching the painting. Will it react with the alcohol? I ask him what the med is. He says it is an antidepressant. I ask to see the bottle. The name ends in "azapine." I tell him sometimes alcohol can be more strong when you're on those. I want to make sure he knows I don't judge him. "I've been on three different antidepressants," I say. "That's how I know."

"A *mzungu* thing," Dianne says later. She means taking meds. She explains that *mzungu* things are things that the colonized people can't know. Like calling codes between countries is a *mzungu* thing. And using hand towels at restaurants before eating.

I tell her about having lunch at a country club when I was eight. It was in Maine. I was raised by casual bohemians on an animal ranch. At the country club we had pea soup with big soup spoons. I slurped. My friend whose father gave us the lunch looked pointedly at me and sipped at the edge of her spoon. I thought I understood. A white people thing.

My friend from home was looked down upon at a wedding for wearing a white dress. I wouldn't have known to tell her not to. When I got a fancy fellowship from a New York foundation, we had a dinner there on 5th Avenue. I wore the embroidered silk pants my film professor handed down to me. My fellow scholarship recipients later told me they knew I was a little different because I wore pajama pants to the banquet. "They were pajama pants?" I said. "Why didn't you *tell* me?"

*

He takes sandals out. Dianne gave them to me. They are beaded leather and different from my normal sandals because they have a lace. She got them in Nairobi.

*

Dianne and I walk now in the cold, wet rainy evening in small-town Quebec a few blocks to the store with palm oil and anchovies. The rain makes its way to my neck.

"Dianne," I say, squeezing her arm, "I was wondering if you and the girls ever felt used by me; I'm worried that this might be something the girls have felt, but not felt like they could say to me."

"Ah," she says, "but sharing my story feels powerful, and that writing is what you do. You are my friend and to know that it is you to share the story makes me feel open and full. If you do something good, there will always be someone to discourage you."

"I want the whole world to know about you," I tell her, and not for the first time. "You and the girls are some of the best people I have ever met. Seeing that you could come through the kinds of things you came through, and choose to have hope and be positive—nothing was the same in my life after that. If I can spend my life writing about you, I will."

*

"Any sharp thing in there that could poke me?" he asks.

"No, no, just another pair of shoes."

Jerk.

.

*

Dianne pretends to be at the keyboard. When she slides into doing impressions it's as natural as a bird who has taken wing at a new angle in its wheelings across the sky.

I realize what I missed once I am back out of Canada. We didn't see any birds. They'd flown south. Usually when I see silos, when I see dawn, when I am in a quiet town, the birds are part of things.

*

He stuffs my belongings back in wrong and then can't zip the yellow bag up without my help. I pray the stitches around the zipper will hold, especially because it's December 18th. Three flights today, prime American holiday travel season, and there's every chance I'll end up checking the suspect mini-mini-mini duffel at the gate.

*

I wrote a little nonfiction book about the girls. About forming an arts group for female refugees and how the women were all from Congo, and how young they were, and how alone and orphaned and wanting of something better they were. How deserving they were. It won no awards; it was what it was. There was no ethical way to write the sort of masterpiece this millionaire writer prowling around the UNHCR was going to write, and that's because none of those people were his friends. He was matter of fact about that exploitation. I was less at peace with mine. With the fact that writing about women who had been gang raped and left to die by the men who slaughtered their family in front of them is necessarily a form of poverty porn, disaster porn, of getting some sort of voyeurism out of the suffering of black bodies. Of participating in the white savior industrial complex. Alexandra Fuller is the only white writer I know who can write about her specific experience in Africa without either avoiding her privilege or apologizing for it, and she grew up there.

133

*

I notice that I look like a few miles of rough road in that self-taken picture at the passport kiosk. I wonder if he saw it on his computers and thought, I'll stop *her*. She looks haggard and under the influence. I was no longer; we'd finished the wine at about 1 a.m. and it was now 10 a.m., but I hadn't slept more than an hour or two and I felt sad to be leaving Dianne, who waited until she saw me waving at her through the train window to turn back around, in the hat with the ear flaps that her church gave her and the jacket someone was waiting to give her at the Montreal airport.

*

On the plane, which was her first ever plane, she leaned in to listen to what her brother said —when she says her brother, she could either mean a Congolese man she knew, or her nephew, or her biological brother. The actual brother is much older than she is—she is one of ten children, and her father was fifty when she was born—I don't ask how old he was when he died—he was a pastor, the father—because she couldn't understand what the people said on the plane, what she was choosing between (chicken and rice? Pasta?), so she tried to say exactly what her brother said, though what she was presented with wasn't something she really knew how to eat—and the older brother, too, is a pastor, or fancies himself one, or is one, I can't quite tell, but both Dianne and finally Jaques tell me he is too Christian. I was born the agnostic child of a lapsed Jewish dude and a lapsed Episcopalian dudette, so even the mellower form of Christianity, to Dianne, strikes me as quite intense, so this is interesting, that she'd say her brother was too Christian— the last night with the wine is also with the *ugali*, which is green and mixed with palm oil and onions and garlic that Dianne chops up—

*

She lifts up one of her eyebrows and assumes an attitude with her shoulders as she advises me how to respond to these trolls, her tone low and skeptical as she pretends to look at the women who trolled me, her eyes lightly rolling: "Thank you for your advices, but…"

134

Burn no bridges. That seems to be her maxim although she doesn't put it like that.

*

The tears only come when we're watching the videos. It turns out the interview with her is the only one I have named. That's why I couldn't find it at first. Instead of VID0026 it's "Dianne." By then we've watched Clemence who reportedly went back to Congo. Nana, the youngest, who is married now in Australia. Suzette, the late addition, who now lives in France. Valentine, settled somewhere in South Dakota.

The videos were all taken one terribly rainy day when the water thundered down in pellets from the sky and some boys from a choir group had taken our room reservation. So instead the girls laughed and laughed and talked, and I took a minute or two of video of each. It's been over four years since then, and we can't get over how young all of them look. Sofia doesn't have long extensions anymore. Valentine is no longer starving. Now she neither carries herself like a little dude, nor does she look like one.

We watch the video of the first play they dreamed up twice. Her nephew Jaques watches with us.

In fact, one of the members of PEN Kenya who saw the girls perform in 2011, when I founded the group, did try to extort Dianne. This happened three years ago. She tells me as we are buying wine at the supermarket to celebrate her birthday, which will happen once I am gone but the cake for which she wants to have the last night of my visit. She didn't tell me, she says, because she didn't want me to get mad at him, as I would have. He invited her to a hotel. He said she looked like his mother and that he loved her. He pled with her to let him tell her story for his book, and promised her money, lots of money, for such a bestseller. She thought about it for an entire year. She decided that that's not what she wanted.

*

The most nagging piece of creative nonfiction feedback I got about my essay on the survival Girls' 2013 performance in Nairobi was from a recovered alcoholic with precious little social skills. His piece came under constructive scrutiny around how he was presenting the Muslim housekeeper as a character. He complained of being called a racist and skipped the next class, which was my workshop, so I only read this in his written comments, later: that "your work has obviously taken a toll on you. There is evidence of PTSD throughout."

How irritating that he would presume to diagnose someone! And how irritating that however ill-advised he was to do so in writing workshop comments, he was probably right.

*

There are moments when the things that upset me that are not related to my immediate present seem to stuff cotton in my ears so that I can't remember what Dianne has just said.

*

It's when we're sitting at her kitchen table, in the day at the beginning of my visit, and in the night at the end, that she says it. I was not connected to the smile inside me, she says. Then when we talked and worked, I found it inside again where it always was.

*

There are moments when her eyes unfocus, and she looks at the floor.

*

After we ice skate, as we sit removing our skates, her eyes do that. I quickly flip through what might have triggered it. The blades in the skates? The fear of trying something new? The realm of disturbance flipped on by the loved experience of gliding as one has never glided before? How quickly the children were whizzing by and sometimes falling in front of us? The elderly person on the ice when we got there, who'd fallen?

*

I'm so happy, she says softly. I want to cry.
I rub her back.

It's okay, I say. You can cry.

She doesn't. Later when we are walking in the nighttime to pick up some eggs at the supermarket, I ask what her biggest culture shock was.

She says, eyes wide, I want to hug people. Even when I just meet them. I have to remember not to.

We arrive home. Dianne holds up the red felt holiday bag and asks Jaques to guess what's in it. He doesn't know. She shows Jaques her skates and tells him how cheap they were (7.5 Canadian dollars at the thrift store). His reactions are too subtle for me to gauge.

*

The English people, the countries they colonized are better, she says at one point or another. The French colonized countries are a mess.

*

Snow in light flurries outside the Chicago airport. Late winter light. I slept in the sort of sleep that straps you to your seat as the plane takes off. I was aware of being lifted, of being kept there somehow, as Montreal dissipated beneath me. Unbidden comes the memory of Dianne after we skate, if that's the right way to describe when someone else goes into the space where their jaw goes slack and they might cry.

*

In Oregon somewhere, in a mall, there is an ice rink. I am eight. Dreadfully wobbly at first on those cold heavy skates, I learn to falter along without my brother Dan or Dad or my mom or Uncle Bob to hold onto. I am not used to such a painful cold gripping my toes, and after I am done wobbling a while, Uncle Bobby helps me get them off. Uncle Bobby is gentle, gentle with a consistency my own dad lacks, so I wish sometimes— like I wish about Marnie's cigar-smoking dad Timmy and Rachel's Jewish intellectual dad Jacob—that Bobby was my dad. I wish it was Bobby who let me warm my feet on his rolling, hairy belly. I can't remember how many people sail, or falter, around the rink as we sit there and my feet come pickily back to life.

Maybe the rink, where Bobby told me quiet jokes, and I giggled extra hard so he wouldn't stop, was a different one from the rink Dan and I skated away from are dad on while he watched from the side. Bobby had a mustache that even now I refer to, as he did when I was young—as his caterpillar. As I nurse my first broken heart years later Bobby will comfort me, wish me well on my upcoming solo trip to Siberia, remarking mildly that he and his wife Sue would still be right here, doing the same thing, when I got back. He will furnish me with a maple scone that morning, the cocker spaniel between us in the cab of his truck. He will make a joke about the sound of the surf, sipping his mug in his straw hat as the roar of semis colors the air. He will drop me off at a quiet gas station in broad daylight to be picked up by a cousin, then double-back twenty minutes later to ferry me over to a Denny's. Siberia notwithstanding, he'd rather I were at Denny's. He'll press money into my hand before he leaves. He'll call it mad money. He will turn out to be right about the heart thing. It just takes time.

*

Just observe, her voice resounds in my mind, her hands gutting the fish. Her sexy Rihanna haircut as she tells me how to respond to the haters. Thank you for your advices, but...

*

Jaques stands in the doorway before we start drinking wine. Quietly pleased.

He holds up a bag.

Inside there is a pair of used skates.

As my body hurtles away from her, I think about them going together, now, to wobble and fall.

A week later she sends me a video on Facebook messenger. She is standing without help in the middle of the rink. Her brother is filming, which means he must be standing in the middle without help also. In the video Dianne starts forward, then tumbles, and face-plants. After a moment, she looks up with a radiant grin.

*

There were so many rivers, gullies, and trees on the dawn train ride out, the cold morning, a few birds on spare branches, Dianne in her hat, waving, and my body hurtling away from her. I pass farmhouses, fields, and into the city, it begins to snow.

I found it inside again where it always was.

Ulaanbaatar, Mongolia
&
Inner Mongolia, China

FURIOUS
ANGELS:
An Essay on the Poetics of Political Exile

Н Э Г

I got to Ulaanbaatar knowing it would be cold. Knowing the face of Myangaa, the Asia Foundation's driver, his tall boots, his hearty embrace. Knowing the drive into the metallic air of Ulaanbaatar. Knowing the puke and the used condoms on the street outside the new apartment block in which I stay in a spare room. The knobby cot and set of drawers that's already breaking like the ones I got last fall at IKEA in Brooklyn and had to keep fixing with CVS superglue. (I used CVS superglue on my boots. I was that broke.) I wake up knowing the annoying song of the gas trucks, the mountain on the south side of the city past Jargalan Town with a white outline of Genghis Khan's face.

Where a flat-sided steep frowns over the present world,
My elbows rest in sea-gaps
Of orbic tendencies to shape and shape and shape

The body lurking there within thy body,
Carrying even her moonsails.

Thus begins a poem I cobbled together out of lines of text for Professor Arnold Weinstein's Civilization and its Discontents Course years ago. The semester I came home early and did my finals in the waiting room at the UCLA hospital. Weinstein, bless him, let students do creative finals, and all I did those long hours during the heart surgery vigil was read over the assignments plus some of my old favorites—Sophocles, Blake, Shakespeare, Adrienne Rich, James Agee, Emily Dickinson, Toni Morrison, Forrest Gander, Charlotte Brontë—and cobble together the lines that spoke to me. It was all I could do. The found poem ended up having twelve sections, and I called it "The Human Act." For three years the poem slept and now, here, in Mongolia, the lines surface and course inside of me. Perie Longo once said it can take decades to write a poem. I also think it can take decades to read one, that as context shifts and whirlpools, the lines brighten and come alive in new forms, resonant and cyclical and informative:

The sea is not a question of power.
Those clarities detached us, gave us form.

I walk down the stairs of the apartment building in Ulaanbaatar, passing the garbage chute on each landing. About my return this is unexpected: it's the off-the-record moments I remember from my year here, not the glowing achievements or abject failures. The time when I found myself farther west than I usually go on foot, and it was windy and icy and February and I had to go to an ATM but didn't know the lay of the concrete, black-slicked land. When I vomited mutton dumplings into a cafe toilet in hot September and Will made me rice. The time a loud screech and crash in the dead of an otherwise silent night had us both wide awake, though neither knew the other was awake so the bed remained quiet.

Hungry clouds swag on the deep,
The chief inlets of soul in this age.

The driver asked us where he was to go.
'To the end of the world!' I cried.

Tumenulzii is waiting for me with Yoshimoto. I exit the building talking into my little camcorder about why what we (me and my camcorder) are about to go do is important. Mongolian youths stare and snicker at the blondie talking to no one. I live about 100 feet from where I lived last year, and briefly consider tracking down my landlady and trying to wrestle the 200 bucks out of her that she conned me out of. That building is a rust-red magnet. A ghost used to whisper to me through thousands of miles of telephone wires in there. I head into the door above which a yellow sign says "London Pub," holding the camcorder in front of me all the while so we can both see his face when we come in the door.

When I came home, on the abyss of the five senses,
The placenta of the real, boundless as a nether sky
Into the deep, down falling, even to eternity down falling,

And he stands up, looking as young as ever though he's fifty now, delighted even though he is still in his own personal hell in Ulaanbaatar, without his friends and family, without his dialect, without his daughter, without his wife, and nothing has moved, nothing has changed since he got his UNHCR Refugee status a year ago except the man who worked there and knew him left, and he got a year older, and his arthritis is worse and his blood pressure too low—

The hoary element roaring—I have to learn alone
To turn my body without force in the deep element

His friend Natsagdorj translates for Tumenulzii at dinner a few days later, after they've had shots of vodka, and I've toasted with wine, and we've all eaten the cow tongue salad—"He says he realizes now after all this, after three years in Ulaanbaatar without his family, to all of these international organizations, that to them, *we are nothing to them*—"

With that inward listening deliberation
The thirst-perishing man might feel
Who knows the well to which he has crept is poisoned

Tumenulzii is learning English. He goes three times a week. He has a bright pink workbook and is halfway through the exercises. I realize how difficult it must be to distinguish between British and American English; in the intersection at the navy-glassed, slant-topped Ulaanbaatar Bank, he tries to say "turn left" and I realize his British teacher says "turn" quite differently than I do. His Chinese enables him to embrace the hard "r" in the American version. The two workbooks have twenty lesson units in all, and, he explains in Mongolian, right now his teacher is the driver of his English, and he doesn't know how to drive, but when he is done with the twenty units he will be the driver of his own English: here he mimes a steering wheel.

Lowering himself from rung to rung in onehanded swoops,
The bone hands roped with vein.
Seen in the smoke of cannon as in a vision
That the laying on of hands meant literally that.

We sit at a table. Looking at Tumenulzii, who is in a jaunty beret. I think I have found the thing that separates people into two groups: an ability to have blinders, to not think about something, but most essentially, to stop feeling something.

To shut it off, put it away, leave it behind. There are those of us who don't have a choice. We can neither forget nor feel less the pain and joy. It makes us good empathizers. It makes us able to brighten others with our joy. (Those others are sometimes those who like how it feels to be opened and seen but only for a short amount of time.) It makes us susceptible to suicide, both fast and the slow kind with alcohol or any other abyss: we don't have enough plexiglass. We feel too much. We think too much. We tend to die young if we don't find a way to deal with it.

"Light!" says Tumenulzii across the table. "You lighter. I light. You light." He scribbles with an invisible pen.

'Everything in life seems unreal.'
'Except me: I am substantial enough—touch me.'
'You, sir, are the most phantom-like of all: you are a mere dream.'
He held out his hand, laughing. 'Is that a dream?' said he, placing it close to my eyes.

That first night, in the pub with Yoshimoto, he and Tumenulzii ask if I have a boyfriend. Of course, the first visit with a Mongolian, even a refugee who needs your help, will not be about business. I sigh. "No."

They refuse to leave it at that. I wasn't going to talk about this. I was here to do work, regardless of how hollow my waking moments were. But this refugee, so dear to me, and his friend want to talk about my heart.

I want to tell them, I do what immature people do with pain! I make myself the tragic hero! I don't want to write another story like that! I'd rather be quiet!

I tell them as simply as I can in Mongolian: I don't have the right kind of heart.

Tumenulzii speaks rapidly and traces a heart on his stomach and we laugh. He meant the chest.

Yoshimoto translates, "You are an honest girl with a good and kind heart. It makes easy to break your heart. You are too honest and good and kind. You have to learn to be a little bit bad person from Mongolia."—he gestures wryly around.

"—*Tenger tinkher!*" adds Tumenulzii.

"Because the heaven—"

"Blue sky. *Tenger medne.*" Tumenulzii points up.

"The sky knows."

A beat.

"The sky knows that before happiness comes difficulty."

The waitress in her white shirt and black corset sweeps, shuts off the front room lights. We sit, looking into our amber beers.

I have heard of day-dreams-is she in a day-dream now?
Her eyes are fixed on the floor, but I am sure
They do not see it—her sight seems turned in,

Gone down into her heart: she is looking
At what she can remember, I believe;
Not at what is really present.

It's two days after Yoshimoto goes back to Japan that Tumenulzii and I arrive at the restaurant where my old boss took me and Will that warm September after picking us up from the apartment a half-block away. One has to go through a Santa Barbara-architecture style white arch to get into the courtyard for those apartments, north of Sukhbaatar Square and the airline ticketing office.

While we wait for the cow tongue salad and Natsagdorj to arrive, Tumenulzii brings out of his briefcase a sheet of paper and scissors. On the top half of the paper are sentences written in Chinese: the bottom, translated into English. He cuts the first strip of English and hands it to me:

"I do thank you for all the."

Zugeer, I tell him, *Bi bag zereg khiisen.* I didn't do much. I could have done more. I wrote an article about Tumenulzii that ended in how I collaborated with the Freedom to Write Program at PEN America to help get him UNHCR Refugee status. And he got it! And it was a happy ending! And I got to bill myself as a Young White Girl Who Came To Developing Nations, Improving Things! Then, in New York, I found out during a phone call the last week of my five months there that the one with the gentle whisper on the telephone was indeed a ghost: that the particular self presented to me, the one I loved, had either never been real, or had died and been dead for a long time. I'd kept looking for my dead friend in the husk, though, and the husk had been hermit-crabbed by a complete and nasty stranger. He was a higher-up in the literary world and advocated for writers like Salman Rushdie. He had mentored my work from afar as I lived in Mongolia, and he knew I wanted to work for him. He'd known it since before the only time I got to see his office, when his married, forty-seven year old tongue licked my twenty-two year old thighs as I squirmed, delighted and confused and a little drunk, in his office chair after hours. When he said that he'd make room for me in his life during my Mongolia year, I had believed him, simply. I had managed not to see outside the snow-globe on his desk, which did nothing more than entertain him on occasion. I'd thought it was the world.

Meanwhile, I was doing nothing of the Improving sort, just reeling around in narcissism and narrative, applying to graduate schools I couldn't afford and selling books for cash. I was not Improving Anyone's Life, especially my own. I was not doing all I could for Tumenulzii. Even worse than a tragic hero is a hero, of any sort.

And on the bleached bones
You listened to the sobbing wind.
Watch out for her; she can give you dreams.
Whatever place she run from ain't going to be a whole lot
Different or worse than the place she is at.

Tumenulzii says he got the translations from the internet, but the writing is his. I commend him. He cuts off the next strip of paper:

"I plan to write a book to the refugees from the memoirs of writer. Entitled "the search for freedom," subheading is: dedicated to Ming. Should be able to be translated into English, Japanese, and Chinese."

I look at Tumenulzii, his face unblemished by the darkness I know is in his heart, the shadow where his loneliness and hopelessness looms in his body like another body, where the smog gets so thick in the -40 wintertime that everyone coughs outside. *Khereggui,* I tell him. You don't need to. Thank you but you don't need to. I have not done enough.

We dream—it is good we are dreaming-
It would hurt us-were we awake.

Хоёр.

In spite of last Saturday's snow this May is warmer than last May in Ulaanbaatar, regularly in the 70s and 80s. The exchange rate has gone from roughly 1,200 Mongolian *tugriks* per dollar to 1,600, so now the "all boots for 5000t" booth near the Central Post Office on Sukhbaatar Square reads "all boots 6000-8000t." Some things are the same. Across from the Flower Center is the 24-hour (Lies! They mean midnight! This I learned the hard way when it was very cold) mini store with a front room still filled with pastel-colored teddy bears.

A year ago, Tumenulzii would text regularly. I am cleaning my clothes! He'd say. His Mongolian was from Inner Mongolia, so the sounds were different. I've cleaned my house today, he'd text.

A year ago Tumenulzii insisted on buying me a train ticket to Hohhot, the capital city of China's 'Autonomous Region of Inner Mongolia,' to visit his wife and see the home he could never return to.

That son grew to manhood among phantoms,
And side by side with a ghost, puddled his clear spirit,
Then leaped into the void between saturn and the fixed stars—
That silence wherein more deep than starlight this home is foundered.

One revolution round the sun ago, a windy day in early May. Tumenulzii took me to the railway station and bought my ticket. I, for mysterious and totally awesome reasons, was outfitted with not only a Mongolian visa for my fellowship year but a Chinese visa—a year long, multi-entry visa. Gold! And it was easy: just buy a train ticket, get on a train, go to China, and do there what would almost certainly have barred me from ever acquiring a visa had the Chinese authorities known what I was using it for: to visit the home and family of an exiled Chinese dissident.

Behold him, part wakened, fallen among field flowers shallow
But undisclosed, withdraw. Time had stopped there and then for the seed
And nothing had happened in time since, not even him.

Tumenulzii was waiting in a suit to walk me to his young lawyer friend's car.

His wife was strip-searched at the border.

No, wrong order.

He gave me toothpaste and wine for her.

He caused the inside of the cave to be infinite.
Or is it that in starry places we see things we long to see?
Let me die by inches.

As with every time we met on any business, we went to eat after he bought me the ticket. I ordered borscht and Tumenulzii ordered us both tall yellow beers. He was haggard and hungover and missed his wife and child. He meant to leave Ulaanbaatar. He meant to go write somewhere where he could live with his family, out from the reach of the Chinese government. "I just want to be together with them; it's not right to be apart," he said in Mongolian. "And I want to leave here, leave anywhere near China." China, where he lived before the police raided his house and office because of the books he'd written about Chinese government and its corrosion of Inner Mongolian cultural heritage and rights. Where his wife still lives, and, he says, is eager to have me.

The sword was suspended above our heads by a single thread
    which was about to snap.
Lift her head from the depths, the red waves of death
As though it were a ghost traveling a half mile ahead of its own shape.
I have wept through nights, you must know that,
Groping laboring over many paths of thought.

Tumenulzii always noticed when I did not have makeup on and said it looked good. He always noticed my face; when I returned from Hohhot with a rash from some wet-wipe tissue from the train he asked about it and whether I had medicine.

A year ago Tumenulzii had a bare apartment. He'd just moved into it. He'd get beer especially for me. He knew I did not like the usual vodka. The famous and young (Outer) Mongolian writer B would later say matter-of-factly that what Tumenulzii spent hours emotionally telling me—about how Inner Mongolians are misunderstood by Outer Mongolians (and both Tumenulzii and Yoshimoto have said this about Buryat Mongolians as well as Inner Mongolians)—is not true. B admits he is no history expert, but he is very sure of this: his kind of Mongolian does not misunderstand these other kinds of Mongolian.

The water is brilliant and nervy,
Breaking up by her entrance
the fiery mosaic I had been piecing together.
Lest the Phantasm-prove the Mistake—that you can fully appreciate all the
    circumstances of our ruin I must elucidate its cause:
A furious angel nailed to the ground by his wings.

Tumenulzii said his daughter was one of the 10,000 students out of 200,000 applicants to test into the best university in China, so she does not want to leave if he is resettled; will she be able to study somewhere good if he gets a teaching post in the western world?

Into my milky tea Tumenulzii put barley. Which made sense to me, it was like breakfast cereal. The mutton dumplings in his milky tea looked a little like brains. What to do with questions of politics, a system (symptom?) of organization for which brains are responsible, when politics makes off with a body, or forces its flight? The body politic and the bodies therein, shunted and kept apart.

That day Tumenulzii said, I don't like to eat alone. There's no point to making food if you're alone, no fun in it.

That called body is a portion of soul
Which cast the metals into the expanse
To gaze at anagrams of light.

The day of my departure to China. Sunset: an unbelievable rose globe looming above the pregnant building on Sukhbaatar Square.

An incomparable globe. How could such a thing be a ball of fire, light years of vacuum away? It's easier simply to believe those things never happened.

The imaginary whistle blows
Out on this stony planet that we farm

In the land of never happened, on the train to China, I shared a train compartment with three men in jackets. One of them brought a crate of beer. The other two didn't know each other either. The first two talked across from each other when I entered the compartment with Tumenulzii's friend, the young lawyer who loosened his tie in traffic on the way here and who wanted to be sure I got my seat. The third one held my book-heavy pack upright while the last passenger lay down, hands braided like praying.

making the familiar faces of men appear strange, and every One unbared a
Nerve: the wondrous fivewindowed nerve and core. The fat gold fly who sang and
botched against a bright pane within.

Amerik okhin! he said. So we have an American girl on board with us. The lights shut off, shut back on, then dimmed. The grime came off my hands as I adjusted my curtains, curled them in on themselves to see the hanging rose globe.

She opens the grass.
There's no lack of void.
The sweetness of your face is just another threat.
I don't know who we thought we were.

The backpack helping praying one, the first to bed, barefoot, is the one to peer at my page. *Boroo gar,* meaning left-handed, apparently, sounds like rain hand, mistake hand, or both.

The train yawned along, looping like two people taking it slow. Treat yourself gently, came a text message from a friend. Dusky marsh, trees up geometric land formations.

But did that ever happen to us?

Г у р а В.

The economic downturn has not hit Mongolia—and the streets of Ulaanbaatar—the way the rise in gas prices did in 2008. There is no discernible rise in crime, and there are several new tourist-oriented places opening up, like the veranda'd Amsterdam Cafe on Peace Street where westerners and wealthy young Mongolians can drink and be seen. Comely Mongolian women with insect-like sunglasses and trendy handbags loiter outside of the new shopping center in the parisian-style building on the east side of the ubiquitous State Department Store.

I first met Tumenulzii in front of the State Department store after an exiled Inner Mongolian in Queens who had read Tumenulzii's books wrote to me, fresh off the plane in Mongolia for my fellowship year, to find him.

The chasm between the concept of destiny and the horrid lot doled out by social inequalities isn't a new one. Tumenulzii does not feel as though he's meant to be in suspended here in Ulaanbaatar, between the country whose government oppressed him and wherever he will be (we hope, with less and less faith) resettled with his family. I would not argue to those displaced with murdered families, either, that this is part of a larger plan, but I won't, as they say, "go there," though because those words are signifiers, metaphors, not an actual place, I have the mobility to do so (the right papers, one could argue)—there's no "getting round" the dead metaphor we don't hear, and it all becomes trite so quickly.

All the dead voices.
They make a noise like wings.
Like leaves.
Like sand.
Like leaves.

The train-compartment companion with the case of beer asked my name. I had by then switched with one of them so I could be a private island up top.

Min, I said, dropping the g at the end as I had grown hip to doing.

What kind of name is that? They asked in Mongolian.

I tried to tell them a story. On the other bunk the first to sleep was sawing logs. How old was I? Twenty three. I have a daughter who is twenty-four, said the carpenter. Or maybe he was a contractor. He'd been in Ulaanbaatar for three months working on three eighteen-story buildings.

My greatest hobby was making little chapels
Run like quicksilver wheat in the lesions of heated air
Out there where that house is burning,
The bells bruising the air above the crowded roofs.

They asked me if I would drink the beer they gave me. I came equipped with a big bottle of Tiger—though Tumenulzii never chose Tiger if Mongolian beer was available because Tiger is Chinese beer. The guy under me held up a plastic water bottle. To clink glasses? No, to drink—vodka in there, not water. When would I ever learn.

One by one my train friends slept. I scratched in my journal: "It doesn't make sense to me. Not talking about logic or even words, which make music out of the world at their best with enlightened language as objects present themselves, passive and aggressive by turns."

Margaret Atwood wrote a short piece about writing as a paper tent, scribbling on the paper as the dark huge wolves and night closed in. Writing does very little in the face of physical danger, was her point (I thought). Nothing so tangible as construction. Nothing so ineffective as marks on paper.

The houses are broken open like pods in the increase of the sun, and they are scattered on the wind of a day's work, alive and separate in that bell-struck air.

'And what is hell? Can you tell me that?'

My body was hurtling through the nightened molasses of the Gobi Desert and unlike Tumenulzii I had the right papers, so it would not be stopped.

I was going from him to her, from where he waited, working as a translator between Chinese, Japanese, and Mongolian, to where she walked, I would soon learn, around the track of the Agricultural University every day at dusk—and every time she did, she remembered walking that walk every day with him before he left two (now three) years ago.

The fading fires just showed her coming up the long, vacant room
as though out of some trivial and unimportant region beyond even distance.

Hell. Someone, in English, can be "going through" it as well as "in" it. Ulaanbaatar, again, is Tumenulzii's hell. This I know. He wants out as badly as I wanted out of myself when the gentle voice of the ghost that comforted me through the phone when I was mugged one night last May in Ulaanbaatar began to belong to a hissing, swearing stranger I didn't recognize.

I think of Tumenulzii's journey, the one inside his mind, when he went from believing these huge international organizations would help him, to realizing they wouldn't, beyond a certain point. (Why am I only now realizing how rife English is with metaphors for physical movement?) The wells to which we crept, respectively, were poisoned. When Tumenulzii's UNHCR contact was replaced by a surly, suspicious newcomer. When I realized my friend had died within a body that kept breathing. When the tree under which one has repeatedly found shelter suddenly is what is toxic, what is harmful, what then? When the well is poisoned? What then?

I was in a printing-house in Hell
and saw the method with which knowledge
was transmitted from generation to generation,
from his cold-house secret
straight to her too-thick love.

A vulgar comparison to draw. Nothing, of course, approximates the experience of human rights abuse, least of all metaphor. A few days ago, when Tumenulzii was cutting strips of paper in English to show me, one said:

"Now my health is very bad situation and mood."

The next one said:

"You write the articles in Inner Mongolia produced great impact. My readers from your articles about my situation, the write E-mail sympathy and understand me."

When Natsagdorj arrived to translate for me, I said it with difficulty: Tumenulzii should understand that if his wish is ever granted to relocate somewhere far away, the Inner Mongolian community that is financially supporting him, that bought him his snazzy new phone and wallet, will not be replaced. He will be far more without a feeling of community and inclusion, and it is this extreme loneliness which haunts and presses down like a dark cloud upon the chests of any resettled refugee I'd spoken with. I did not want to say this but felt I had to.

Each is a new and incommunicably tender life, wounded with every breath. The human act will make us real again.

T a B a H .

Erlian was dusty, windy, and a little chilly. Against clouded brown air and light fixtures that looked like dandelions, the flag flew at half-mast. The same woman who met my eyes like a hawk when I handed her my bedsheets on board the train then had a talking crush on me in the hallway because of my blue eyes—and then chased me out of the bathroom—passed by, her shift over for the time being. This region, the deserts of China and Mongolia, did feel to me unequivocally like the dusty, barren apocalypse, the real end of the world. During the night sometimes the man in the opposite bunk would sit cross-legged in his paisley long underwear, studying me. Each time it always looked the same out—rock, sand, Gobi, pre-dawn. Now I waited in the cold gusts sitting on my bag on the side of the train station, wondering how to prepare for meeting the family and visiting the home of someone who had been exiled.

I tried to make my eyes blaze with other fires than those of love,
With corroding fires, or whistle's echo, sinking, sunken.
Tell him... tell him you saw me and that... that you saw me.

A team of forest-green-suited police were there to greet us when the train arrived, standing between the train and log-laden cars on the next track. They shone flashlights on the floor and roof of the train hallway, felt my bed nonchalantly, asked me for an entry card I was never given, then shrugged and walked away. Now they filed into a van. Would they have taken him into that van if he had attempted to return to his wife and daughter.

You have rather the look
of another world.
We have our reasons.
How could you leave the crime uncleansed so long?

I thought I should not blink once, because I was in the land that was only a dreamscape to him: he would never come back, and as a place his body would never reside, it was now, to him—to his brain in the body whose mobility was and is limited by political restraints—strictly a world of metaphor.

I waited. Pushy taxi drivers. A woman with a gauze scarf pulled over her face, smushing her features. Tumenulzii called me on my phone, which got service there, to say to stay where I was. Tumenulzii's friend, who picked me up after a while, was a doctor with an office in one of the spaces of a mall, a sort of deserted outlet place. The other spaces in the warehouse sold all manner of things but mostly cheap clothing. There was a picture on the wall of a wolf and a Chinese emperor guy. Calendars. When I asked what kind of *emch* (doctor) he was, he pointed to them.

You cannot explain to others because they have no conception of what is meant.
They say they are ions in the sun.
You may say it is to prevent our reason from foundering.

His wife mopped the floor. A sterile smell. Their daughter, an eight year old in a pink shirt, black pants, and clackety black flats scurried by, a white mop dog in her arms. She played jump rope with a long, rubber rope in the wide warehouse hallway with the other girls. Some of them sat and whispered on the sofa next to me, finally asking me how old I was. I slept and woke in a place that was not supposed to be surreal—not a metaphor for me—vibrating white light and girls clacking and jumping rope. The mother and daughter put on their jackets and left. The light was never direct. There was too much dust for that.

The book Tumenulzii is writing now, he indicated through Natsagdorj when we met for dinner, chronicles his journey from China to Mongolia. I can't wait to read it—to be able to read it in Mongolian or to read the English version, whichever comes first—because those moments in Inner Mongolia were, for me, peppered with holes in the narrative. Flickering in and out of sleep in that strange room in the storehouse mall, I wondered, was this a friend who helped him escape? Did he need help escaping, even? How much time did he have, or felt he had, to leave? How much time passed between when the police raided his house and his office, and did he know they would come? If he did not have such negative associations with the Chinese government, would he long for home? What thoughts did Tumenulzii's inner world churn out as he left his country of birth?

Look the house in its blind face.
the Film upon the eye
had the opal lightings of dark oil.
Winging, swept away,
What good were eyes to me?

The car was taking four people to Hohhot and I was the first, which meant I got to see the bright shapes of Erlian's buildings against the dusty air as we made the rounds to hotels to
pick the others up.

In the car on the way to Hohhot every red flag flew at half-mast. The three men I rode with, I knew, made up the miracle of the present but I still did not want to talk to them. Dinosaur statues on the way into Hohhot, twenty of them sweeping the landscape over hundreds of yards. *All is well in the world*, read some meditations. *Life is unfolding as it is meant to.* A chorus of schoolchildren were trapped under buildings for a third day then, in the aftermath of the Sichuan earthquake. Dust formed a globe of the sun. It always would. "Stew in the screen of the mind," I scratched. First a flat expanse, then rows of trees thrashing, then as it grew dark the great sleeping-boar shape of a mountain.

The words are purposes.
The words are maps.
I myself but write one or two indicative words for the future.

They dropped me off first. I said thank you to the moon, hanging full above their apartment. The first thing I noticed was how much less tired, how much happier, the face of Tumenulzii's wife was as I glimpsed it through the window before exiting the taxi; I had seen her once before, in Ulaanbaatar, when she had just arrived for a visit from Hohhot the previous night. Here she was happy and affectionate—why wasn't she like this before? Was she exhausted from the train ride she had taken the day before from Hohhot to Ulaanbaatar? Was she worried? Had she been detained again? I knew the swiss-cheesed narrative, the lack of information and data and fact, influenced my experience there, as one that played out almost exclusively in subjective, emotional terms.

Facts are not always mine to obtain, though; I didn't know *how* to be there. I didn't know the words to all these questions. Plus her dialect, the Inner Mongolian, as it contrasted with the Outer I learned, made even the most basic communication difficult. I didn't know if the questions were appropriate to ask, or even if it was safe to ask them in that apartment.

She persuaded us to let the mystery go
And concentrate on what lay at our feet.
The worst of words. The original quarry, abyss itself.
You need riches, armies to bring that quarry down!
Will you swallow, will you deny them, will you lie your way home?

The walls were turquoise. She sat across from me. She worked today; it was Monday and she was a geography teacher. She mixed sweet yogurt and grain, gave me milky tea and a can of beer, cut the mutton for me from the bone when I showed myself to be incompetent. The mutton was the best thing I had ever tasted and I'd sworn I was done with mutton. I looked at her face and at her daughter's room, where I would sleep. *This is where he cannot be. This is where he cannot be.*

It is weak and silly to say you cannot bear what it is your fate to be required to bear.

24 hours later, after a day of outings, she let down her hair and it framed her face.

If they were to reunite, would they fit together again? With the death of the gentle ghost's voice that comforted me on the phone during my year in Mongolia, with the replacement of that self I loved by an unkind stranger, I learned it's possible for a self one loved to die while its body, the shell, lives on and grows new selves, nothing like the ones before. What if this happened to Tumenulzii and his wife? When distance is chosen—or, in the case of an exile, forced—experience of an other becomes dependent on medium, which doesn't cover everything. All sorts of changes can occur. The body lurking within a body—hope, optimism, a self—can die, and the other doesn't always know. What of realignment, should they be allowed to reunite?

You have not wept at all!
I see a white cheek and a faded eye,
But no trace of tears. I suppose, then,
Your heart has been weeping blood?
I have always stood in the way of your pleasures.
Open your eyes. Look and see who I am.

In Hohhot's new Museum of Inner Mongolia they already had a graphic design poster with images of the Sichuan earthquake. The museum also boasted the largest complete dinosaur skeleton in the world. The guide accompanied us for it though she knew nothing about it since she was actually stationed on the floor below, and she wouldn't shut up, so I retreated until she left. I call Tumenulzii's wife *Mother* in Mongolian, *Eej*, and accordingly, it took me no time to become the sullen daughter. *Eej* alternately pushed and pulled me by the elbow and I, sleepy from the day and a half of transit to get there, felt irritated and unable to help feeling irritated.

Sometimes the body is a heavy thing to lug; it was for me when I knew I was walking in the nightmare of Tumenulzii's memory, China, but also in the miracle of his hope, in the form of his wife. She took the day off to spend with me there in the museum, where the stuffed inanimate animal skins all looked vaguely confused.

Witness, you ever-
burning lights above, who are so
lovely fair and smellst so sweet
that the sense aches at thee:
Suppose we repented.

161

All over Hohhot streets, taxi screeches—in the restaurant thank goodness I came awake though I *shuvuu shig iddeg* ("eat like a bird")—only the mind and its attachments form the specters—I like this hour, I tried to tell her: the most popular Mongolian restaurant in Hohhot and we are the only customers—waiters walk by singing, and towards the back the cooks sleep with their heads in their arms—bed on the verge of breaking— futile to want the connection dreamed of, in which one does not construct oneself but one simply *is*—the cottonwood leaves clappered outside—a tea set shaped like genitals in the museum—a cup of coffee in "Mike Dong," as she said: McDonalds (and there is not one Mike Dong, KFC, or Starbucks in all of Outer Mongolia)—taxis like a school of fish outside the train station— they gave you a large faux-denim backpack in which to put your purse, then they lock it with a sensor for the duration of your stay in the bookstore—in the front of the museum a huge piece of topaz that supposedly looked like an eagle, which supposedly looked like the state of Inner Mongolia—the museum was huge, new, built in 2007, so Tumenulzii hadn't seen it—behind his house, the university track field, where kids run around at dusk, playing ball—fewer people in Hohhot than in Ulaanbaatar, but Hohhot is worlds more developed—clean, wide streets, like a Chinese Seoul—women taxi drivers—this is one way political privilege seeps through the cultural script of literature: I could confuse the past and present tenses, I could switch voices, whereas Tumenulzii's past and present were starkly divided, and the violations had happened to him and his wife and will always have happened to him and his wife, not a "you" they can separate from—

Give me the ocular proof, if only to save you from freezing at the street corner all
night, to comply with heat: Bells in your parlors, wildcats in your kitchens;
After every tempest come such calms. Even then this forked plague is bated to us.

This, however, is one thing I choose to keep present whenever it rises up in me: outside, on the university field, a candlelight vigil is being held on the concrete track. On the ground the candles form the shape of a heart. It is for the earthquake victims. It is where Tumenulzii and his wife would walk at dusk.

Repented what?
Our being born?
Remorse is the poison of life.

З у р Г а а h.

Tumenulzii's niece and nephew arrived during breakfast. I could see Tumenulzii in his nephew's eyes. The nephew was twenty according to himself, nineteen according to his sister. He put mutton in his milky tea; she put cheese in hers. She was, of course, perfect, hair in a swept side ponytail.

I don't edit my texts as well as I should before making them available, but some of the grammatical/editorial mistakes are actually intentional. Example: "Would they have taken him into that van if he had attempted to return to his wife and daughter." The padded throne of textual space (here we go again, English and its movement) allows me this method of driving home (ditto) an emotional point (ha!). On the page, i.e. in the land of mimicry, I can mimic a question that does not turn up at the end—many languages do not turn up their questions at the end, including Mongolian. In these houses of questions and constructions of politics, pages are freedom-spaces and also very weak—hence, and bring on the metaphor (bring it: bring it from there to here)—the oft-used comparison of thin walls to paper.

Should I be surprised, then, that conversations with a tender ghost over wires during my year in Mongolia enabled my friend to turn into a ghost without my knowing just how dead and gone (from here to a there I can't see) my friend was? Just how forced out of my best friend I had been, and would continue for long painful months to be. Tumenulzii has adjusted to the idea that protection is fleeting. Should I be surprised that at physical approximation, the tree under which I took shelter, the well I used to drink from, was poisoned?

What if
a man went into his house and leaned his hand
against the wall and the wall
was not?

When Tumenulzii and his wife lived together, did they hurt each other? Did they fight? What does the strain of exile do? Is abstraction the worst kind of decoy. Is it more toxic to meet and cause pain where love once lived, or to leave that stone unturned and continue as the ballerina rehearsing every moment for a recital she'll never give—in the case of Tumenulzii and his wife, the chance to live together again in bodily proximity.

Better than any description of buildings or garments,
The theory of a city, a poem,
With iron and stone edifices, ceaseless vehicles,
As a matter of decent of form rather than rebellion—
Formed a heaven of what he stole from the abyss.

Tumenulzii's niece and nephew took me back to the museum, to the third-floor displays of song and dance traditions and hilarious Chinese translations. A sunny day outside, a day that took forever to get started— the niece's knock was assimilated into my dream as someone knocking on a car window—to lunch where they kept ladling food out of the hotpot, and I realized I just had to say no thank you and let the food pile up, all green, and the beer opening like a gunshot. The teacher who ate with us knew enough English to explain the train back to Mongolia to me: first a ten-hour layover then a four or five-hour one. I told them I would sleep and read during the ten-hour layover rather than disturbing the doctor and his family again; they wouldn't hear of it but I was adamant. That evening *Eej* fried up our leftover green beans with meat and rice.

It's not good to eat alone, she says, exactly as Tumenulzii had before, in another country, down to the very inflection.

Ship and towered city are nothing,
Stripped of men alive within it, living as one.

On the way home from the park, T-shirts hanging, people eating at barbecue stands. Tumenulzii calls *Eej* while we walk but something is wrong with the cell phones. I kept thinking of the word trick Godisnowhere. She insisted on coming to the park. I had wanted to go run alone instead of being pulled and cattled—we saw a movie and I let her pull me along after, trying to adjust for a few hours to the closeness and steering.

She wanted to change my mind about the train layover. I live alone in Mongolia, I said, to which her response was that my ten-hour layover would be me alone in China. The park had it all, teenagers playing ball and a group of middle-aged power-walkers. Young hip couples wrapping arms about each other, girls with mullets, all in skinny jeans. I used to come here with Tumenulzii, she said. We would walk for an hour together every night around this time and talk.

Picking out our way through verbs and ruins,
That single idle word blown from mind to mind.

Tumenulzii called the apartment, and when I talk to Tumenulzii on the phone my voice always goes up a register. He asks if the trip was good, if she was feeding me. No actually, it's possible that I don't remember what he asked, I only know what he would ask, given the small pool of words I could understand.

His blood began again, talking and talking.
Did the letters work upon his blood?

What did you talk about? I asked fifteen minutes later after I jogged the track while she walked it. His writing, she said. Literature. In the little sector of woods between the university buildings and the apartment buildings in which she lived and Tumenulzii used to live, she wended through the trees only to turn at the curb and enter them again. I uncovered what I half-felt before, of my role is as medium, that there was no experience I had that year that was not to write about—though that's not exactly right—man did the air smell good on that little path—

The breastlike, floral air is
the bloody tribute we had paid that harsh, brutal singer
at the deadest hours of the night.
At each stroke blood spurts from the roots.

166

A cheerleader-style gaggle of girls, teens on the bleachers, two on the track learning to rollerblade. She walked, looking back periodically to check on me as I stretched. I asked if I could look at the vigil underway in the center of the loop of track. Fewer candles than yesterday: flags back up from half-mast.

A girl approached shyly in fits and starts with two lit candles to where *Eej* and I stood at a distance. Please come, she says to me, little with big eyes.

Eyes going and going,
A swirl of it, nerves and clots,
Can roar in the heart of itself as a symphony,
Perhaps as no symphony can.

The students all looked like Brooklyn hipsters, leggings, mullets and all. They sang a Chinese nationalist song. I didn't realize how scarce foreigners were in Hohhot. They were agricultural university students. After I joined the circle I saw that the candles set upon the ground on top of the Dixie cups spelled something, but I didn't know any Chinese besides thank you, so when the kids speaking and holding papers said something about me I didn't know until all dark eyes turned my way. A tall boy came and stood next to me when the pixie girl couldn't quite understand me nor I her.

"Say what you feel, about the earthquake," he said.

"I am here to—" I began in a small voice—

"—Speak to everyone," he encouraged.

I looked up at the eyes.

"I am here to honor the spirits of the dead and grieve with you," I said.

"Thank you," they said together.

We stood holding our candles in our Dixie cups.

Whatever is neglected slips away.
You elements that clip us round about,
All sent back by the echoes:
Heaven has always chosen the time.

The next morning the niece took me out again. In the park, crowded with people and children for whom many empty kiddie-rides trundled round and round, incredible amounts of pollen tufts fell and drifted along like piano notes. A girl sang her heart out in the very corner of the park, next to piles and piles of shingles. A little boy fished in a shallow pool. Haughty looks from those power walkers. Less than 48 hours there in Hohhot; it took longer than I spent there to train there and back, listening to the groan of wheels on track as the lines coursed through me, looped an infinite number of times.

All times mischoose.

The night I left *Eej* and her niece stood outside the train window, as did the families of the other three passengers in our compartment. We crowded round. One of my compartment companions looked immediately to me like a band member—the loose half open shirt, the shaggy hair longer in back—and I would feel worse about profiling him if I hadn't turned out to be right. He was an opera singer, actually, coming to Ulaanbaatar for a show. A man with a cigarette in his mouth and similar hair and face to the opera singer came to the window, grinning.

"Your little brother?" I asked.

"Yes."

Somewhere in this train car was a former student of *Eej's*. When she said she was a geography teacher, she explained that she teaches what people of different regions eat, wear, (here they have sheep, she gives as an example, but in Argentina they don't, because it's too hot). Her student came in where I was miserable in my just woke up and unable to move state—had no sense of the hour; we were in the huge warehouse where they change the bogeys on the bottom of the train at the Mongolia-China border and the clangs resounded.

The boss was dead, the mistress nervous and the cradle already split.
I did what human beings do instinctively when
They are driven to utter extremity—looked
For aid to one higher than man.

They all slept as my body trundled along with them to Tumenulzii and a land of relative freedom of speech. Sunrise all to myself. Had seen the pink along the horizon for a while, then the gold bar, milking around flush with the horizon.

I fished in the cardboard box *Eej* packed with a week's worth of food for me, hoping to find that one apple. When I looked up again the sun was a rectangle of gold light with rounded corners. I watched it detach like an egg from an ovary under a microscope as in that video kids in some countries are made to watch. Burns on my retina exact as hole puncher detritus. Realized after a while of staring at it that I could only do so because the sun-spot of burn had layered over what I stared at.

Is reform needed? Is it through you?
No message plucked from the birds, the embers.
Always a knit of identity,
The moon had opened a blue field in the sky.

Had I written the right things down? What to absorb but impressions, since information was dependent on time (too short) and a knowledge of the habits of Chinese authority (nonexistent) and a cultural sensitivity to journalistic questioning, not to mention language barriers? I abandoned the effort; the one fact I knew was that I needed someone, and maybe she did too. Someone there in the warm flesh. By the end I leaned into her and waited to be taken along by the elbow.

Where's my voice?
Where are all these corpses from,
Scattering too some heavy
Unwelcome thoughts that were beginning to throng on my solitude?

Before falling asleep the grandpa of the compartment asked me to sing. They'd tossed back a few, I think, this motley crew of new friends. They really were strangers at the outset of this journey, but by morning they were all getting off the train together to eat, buying each other and me *tarag* and water, and in Erlian, big boxes of fruit because fruit was so much cheaper there than in Ulaanbaatar. The opera singer, who refused to sing last night now was humming in head phones, looking down at sheet music. Everyone took off to eat in the sunshine. The doors to the train station were set to open at 2 p.m., and by 1:30 p.m. there were mountains of canvas bags and boxes in front of the station doors and a long line of passengers waiting sensibly in the shade of the line of trees across the parking lot. Bright geometric shapes, wider roads than Ulaanbaatar, actual intersections.

Intersections, coincidentally, are one of my favorite metaphors once they make the leap from the outer world to the inner one.

What do you do
when you fall far from help? Night doesn't fall. Left to myself I abandoned myself:
I think the sun where he was born drew all such humours from him,
For he only holds a candle in the sunshine.

I couldn't wait to see Tumenulzii and show him the photos I had taken of his family, couldn't wait for him to make the leap from the inner world of my mind to the Outer world of his hell, Ulaanbaatar. I was selfish in that way, perhaps. It wasn't my hell. My hell would take another year to darken the walls of my mind. In his lectures Professor Weinstein said with great feeling that a central message to the texts he used, the texts that buoyed me through the hell of the heart surgery waiting room vigil and which buoy me now as I do my best to bury the tender ghost I loved who disappeared—during the phone call when I realized the voice didn't belong to my friend anymore the professor's words came back to me—*"the prison in which you live is of your own devising"*—

The thing I came for: the wreck
and not the story of the wreck.
You won't hear it nicely. If it hurts you, be glad of it.

And, with respect to my situation, not Tumenulzii's, he might be right. There is a core selfhood that should not be given out to another body, since

170

the self within that body might disappear without its husk disappearing as well. But love dissolves the plexiglass, which is why hissing and swearing hurts more when it comes out of a body that used to house a friend—it goes right in. I crouched sobbing with my phone to my ear at the corner of 103rd and Broadway, clear in the all-clicking-into-place that around that time last year, when I went to Hohhot, my friend had died, but I'd kept thinking my friend was in there somewhere, looking for him and getting hurt every time I did, and I will always prefer to have sobbed rather than swear and hiss back at the stranger who took over the husk.

It is very late in the day to offer me your tears.
Now about setting you free:
I cannot fall because there is no room to.

The trick to this burial, I think, is to recognize the presentation of self as a vessel of words into which I poured love—love that was nonetheless real. Recognize that if there wasn't something real about that which is presented with words, language may never have evolved.

Of course anything dependent on language (like a correspondence over wires by two selves inside bodies separated either, as in Tumenulzii's case, by force, or in my case, by the choice of one) is bound by its limits. How can I grieve for my best friend when the physical subject-markers that humans use to melt plexiglass with those they trust are still there: face, eyes, hands.

My related question: What is the psychology of adjustment for people who are exiles? Did Tumenulzii need, on some level, to bury his wife in order to move forward in his life without her, even as he knew there was a (smaller and smaller) chance they'd be together for longer than a week again?

Rescue yourself, your city, rescue me—
Rescue everything infected by the dead.

"Prison", "torture," and "exile" are big catch-words in a vocabulary ridden with them. Power and authority are endemic to the English language, but the same is arguably true of language in general. I escaped upstairs in the train station, since I had no physical cargo besides my body, which was equipped with the right paper. A windowless, customerless, duty-free shop up there, all cigarettes and booze. While the ant hill subsided downstairs I talked with a friendly Australian about how my desire to learn Chinese had subsided once I realized the rote memorization necessary to learn an alphabetless language.

How can I say things that are pictures:
To say be kinder to yourself.

We stopped in Zamin Uud and none of the Australians knew what *kimch*i was—this was after the dominatrix train employee ordered people off their bunks when she looked at their passports. It was the hour it grew dark, so after paying the dollar-to-use bathroom on the central square similar to one in a central Mexican town, we wandered away. Split level buildings that reminded me of my hometown in California, young people hanging out on the stoops. We found a square brown brick building with a karaoke room and a bar in the basement, a supermarket and a restaurant on the ground floor, and a kid's playground on the second floor. When we left it was dark, 8 p.m., and I saw the slim silhouette of a child watching us from a second-floor window.

The earth abode of stones in the great deeps,
the only name I have for you, that, no other—ever, ever, ever!

By now my dishonesty, I hope, is obvious. Obvious that on the level that matters—as in, physical matter! metaphor, will conceptualization ever be free of you?—but anyway, obvious that on the level that matters: there *are* no poetics to exile. Not the exile which is not metaphorical. Or if there are, Tumenulzii is the only one with access to his. Discourse is shredded as easily as paper when it comes (comes. from here to there.) to these issues: there are no heroes in this text, there is no perfection, and Tumenulzii's story isn't finished. I try to be kind to myself: metaphor evolved perhaps because it is inextricably intertwined with empathy.

In other words, if I did not have my own admittedly small-minded story of dislocation and estrangement from a beloved other, of grief, with which to understand Tumenulzii's narrative through one of its many holes, I perhaps would have noticed even less of what was important.

I treated *Eej* to the ever-rare trip to a cinema. We saw the animated flick *Iron Man*. Her delight at going to the movies and her hand steering my elbow: that was important.

When Tumenulzii picked me up from the train and made sure I got home, when we met up later and he said for the second time to the word exactly what his wife had said days before, in another country (that of memory, now) 5 p.m. honey light lighting up the sun of his face: It's not good to eat alone.

That was important.

In rooms of selfhood where we woke and lay watching
today unfold like yesterday, we had to take the world
as it was given. The human rose to haunt us
everywhere, raw, flawed, and asking more than we could bear.

(How was it we were caught?)

Syktyvkar, Russia

LENIN

I.

Outside a block of flats, a group of children. A boy circles on a bike. His companions chase and laugh. On the second floor, a man stands on a balcony and smokes. A woman leans out of the fourth floor, shakes a rug, recedes. The wall is huge, with orderly windows and stacks of balconies. The wall swallows the woman and her rug.

No, not even that.

The brunette woman and her red rug. They were never there.

II.

Anya and I walk in the fog to the canteen. I remind myself to go faster; she is always waiting for me. We take off our coats and scarves and hand them to a woman in a blue apron. She gives us dirty plastic tags. The old guard kicks his feet up on the desk. I am learning to fix my hair in the mirror like Anya does, though mine doesn't have the flip she blow-dries in hers each morning. Thick, warm juice. Boiled cabbage. Fish. Cream globs on the surface of my soup. It is here I look at her face. The walls are pink.

Outside, litter. The curtains are frilled. Outside, birches just now bare and stained with rain. I watch her everywhere we go. At twenty-seven, she has no particular wish to be somebody's wife. I look at her shapely buttocks in tight pants as she buys tickets for the Board of Trustees' trip to Finland. She earns a good salary. Her voice is soft.

Even in Objachevo, a village of 8,000, there is a Lenin. He is silver and pointing. I can see why men prayed to him. I want to discuss the irony of this with someone, but I have already plied my English-speaking friends with too many questions, and so far I only know enough Russian to say Thank you, I'm full.

What would Lenin point at? The future, maybe, though on such a brilliant morning, silver finger afire, the future is too abstract of an answer. A particularly graceful birch tree leaking yellow onto the pavement? A stark land, northwest Russia, forest as far-reaching as grief. Thank you, I'm full.

III.

Around us business people in dyed red hair or ill-fitting suits are taking their lunches, looking seasick under the fluorescent light. Anya nudges me, says the man in back and to my left is Ludya's boyfriend. Which one? The married one. I have no idea what constitutes an appropriate glance. The instant I look, he is biting down on a roll. The reel of film plays over and over, the mechanical lift of the arm, eyebrows working down with the chomp, over and over, grinding into Ludya's thin, bronze body, over and over. Grimacing the way someone taking a bite does. Over and over. A business suit sleeve and a roll glazed with sugar. No face. Just a bite.

The stairwell smells like sulfur. Empty cigarette packs and fish heads on the steps. I hurry up eight flights, hoping to somehow stave off the meatball weight gain, shedding layers of clothing as I go, remembering half the time to be conscious of dark corners. The words "hip-hop" are written in English on the walls. Windows are broken. A window of the staff van was broken during just one night in Objachevo. When a window is broken the conclusion is always that someone was drunk.

176

Anthropology 140: Cultural Anthropology. The lecture is about the political lives of dead bodies. Lenin's body in particular. It was moved a few times. I listen. Quickly cease to remember. We discuss statues. Immortalizing people. The philosophical meaning of Lenin's statues. He is everywhere. His face is godly. He is dead. He is worshipped. His body a political symbol, its movement a political statement.

Russia in my mind is a dreary place, cold, wide, unintelligible. Solemn. Frightening. I leaf through the class text, imagining other humans endowing a corpse with meaning as a sort of collective ball of light, a 5 o'clock p.m. honey light, behind the head of the corpse. The audience wowing at a product of their own wishing. Like the quark machine at Princeton someone told me about once. Not very many quarks recorded while no one was there. If someone came, sat, looked at the screen, wanted quarks, there they were. There is Lenin, handsome, a man of the people. Peasants crowded round his deathbed.

The head cashier notices me the first time we come to this particular canteen. She has a large mole and sharp eyes. I only need to learn once how she reacts to my not eating everything on my plate to subtract the heavy potato from my selections and dutifully gobble the rest. She comes to fill the salt shakers and checks my progress, nods, says something to Anya. At my request, Anya translates. She says you're a good girl.

IV.

Time behaves strangely, swallowing events. The puddles have frozen but cars still rush between potholes and swerve dangerously. It is an odd feeling, these Russian mornings, these dirty buses. I am everywhere. I am nowhere. I am stretched between people. Women trudge, shawls around their heads, crossing themselves fervently at the gate of a brand-new Byzantine church. I walk past a park filled with birch trees to a warm office where there is tea in the kitchen and aerosol room freshener in the bathroom. My daydreams are vivid enough to be happening somewhere: on the day of my father's death the man I love lies in bed with me, looking at my face.

The Russian word for *car* sounds to my untrained ear like the Russian word for *men*.

We all know it is one of the last clear days of autumn. I am about to experience my first Russian winter, but there is no trace of it in the broad sky and river. Stout, golden light. Birches half-naked and still. We roast sausages over the fire, celebrating the weather with a picnic of equal parts meat, potatoes, and alcohol. The factory across the river leaks smoke like ink in cursive across the sky's pale edge. Vladimir's favorite soccer team, St. Petersburg's club team, won yesterday. He belts out its anthem on the steep riverbank, spilling his oddly colored drink. Lena adjusts her quiet toddler's hat. Ludya redoes her lipstick. Sasha and Anya joke in a language I still don't understand. It sounds like they are rolling marbles in their mouths. As long as I am a stranger in a strange land, I decide, drunk, I have no choice but to hibernate in the den of my internal world.

Sasha bundles little Lucia in his jacket with his big hands. She fell into the water. She sniffles. Vladimir undresses a birch limb with his knife. The shavings fall like snow.

V.

I read *Einstein's Dreams,* in bed with my first Russian cold. We cannot know the nature of time; we live according to its nature. Time could go in a circle. We might know. Time could be a sense. We wouldn't know. The cigarette I have longed for all afternoon is in my hand, the railing of the front steps dirty and bent and too cold to touch. A huge machine pounds cement stakes into the ground in the next plot, which shakes our building to a slow rhythm—a giant approaching, screaming maiden in his fist.

I walk beside Andrei, thinking of a quote: "The soul of another is a dark forest." (Who wrote that? A Russian did.) His dark forest like a sphere around his head and body, pathways of solids and fluids, thought and matter. The lines of our lives touch like moths, stretch parallel on a damp street. Which dimension is it that has us seeing everywhere we've been? The first snow falls and barely sticks, dusts the tops of logs. Women in fur hats glance curiously. His face fraught with acne. He tested well enough to go to Moscow to study physics, but he must stay here. He does not live in a flat. He lives in a wooden house with electricity but no hot water, taking care of his mother, who works at a telegraph center. He never knew his father. He has drawn up a list of questions in English to ask me.

"The soul of another is a dark forest." Quotes validate writing, supplement, elucidate. Supposedly. Quotes depend on the past. They emerge out of it as out of a deep pond. Goldfish, at least, do not pretend to have enough of a grasp on the past to thrust greedily into a context. A life. Emerge triumphantly with something to gut. The body of Lenin is empty of vital organs. It is currently being dressed in a new uniform by people in a laboratory. A good quote illuminates an essay, gives it a back. Good lighting illuminates Lenin's husk to make him look godlike.

According to Anya, Lenin has no back. Andrei would like to read my poetry. When it is time to leave I say Thank you and he does not respond. I say Thank you again and he says I do not know what to say. I say Maybe you're welcome. He looks at me, thinking. Those are common things. I like to say original things but I do not know enough English. He shuts the door. Lenin's body imitates that of a saint, liberated (or restrained) from natural decomposition.

Look closely at Lenin's mouth. How easy it would be to open it, fingers working the cold skin (stubble?) and place the apple there (teeth?). I wonder what it is like to own a brain that devotes itself to the consideration of atoms, neutrons, magnetism. Andrei certainly does not know enough English to tell me *that*. Which dimension is it that has us seeing everywhere we've been?

VI.

When I am six I teach myself to tie my shoes, waiting on a railroad tie for my mother and brother to come out to the car. In Russia they keep the original soundtrack under the voice-overs, so British movies aired on Russian channels sound like crowded airport bars. I am two, telling my sister I don't want her to cut my food, I want Daddy to, and Daddy complies. At the bottom of a Russian glass of juice there is solid fruit, which one spears with a fork. I am eighteen, and a boy with dark hair asks me quietly in a restaurant in Montreal if we can have our first kiss. Russian schoolgirls walk arm in arm in pink jackets, long braids down their backs. I am fifteen and I tell my father I don't think he should shout at his doctor just because the doctor might not give him his Vicodin; my father pulls over and leaves me by the side of the road.

The organization I type English documents for is dedicated to implementing sustainable forestry. The biggest obstacle is turning out to be changing the mind of the local population, teaching them the process of democratic determination when they are used to a Soviet state issuing orders that are not questioned. Convincing them that they have a voice. Teaching them how to use it. Old-growth forests are protected now, according to agreements between scientific institutions, logging companies, and the people. The soul of another is a dark forest. The soul. A forest. Does this mean we are reforming how a soul works? Protecting its untouched parts. Reforming. Are we saving souls?

VII.

Anya takes me to visit her parents. I can't tell if the shouting and breaking is normal until Anya sits on the edge of the bed I have been napping in, tears in her eyes. I am sorry, she says. I didn't know things had gotten this bad. It is our first time alone together outside of the office. I want her to like me. Shouting and breaking happened in my childhood home, too. I am lonely. I touch her shoulder. Her mother comes in, speaking unevenly in Russian. A cigarette dangles from her hand. She lifts the other hand, strokes my forehead in jerks. My feeling has no name. This touch belongs to Anya. I ache to lean into it; I have not been touched this way in years. We leave early, I look out the window, the sky opens with rain. We are superimposed over each other, with intention and without. We do not accept touch according to script. Is this the one conclusion? There is this longing. Our weeping is out of sync. The sky opens with rain.

180

I am nineteen, shaping my face like clay. I am twenty-two, at my first job, nervous.

Lenin died in nineteen twenty-two.

This from Sasha, and not a fact I bother to check. I give my Russia to the people I meet to shape like clay.

I lied, I do check, and the year the book says is not the year Galina sitting up straight in her chair eyebrows knit remembers it being.

VIII.

According to records, someone broke my heart. My own words become a quote, then, in the onion of remembering. I walk across a street I sound out with a clumsy foreign mouth: *Katoovskaya Treenadtset*, parting the air of an outer layer. A layer where someone broke it but it is not broken. No, not even that. If there is no break. How can one claim it was broken?

Lenin to my right, eyes forward as soldiers. The past replaced.

The past effaced.

The past retraced.

The past erased.

And it is never someone, really. Not, at least, when we are nineteen. We are all too alone together for that. You broke your own heart. The sky is cranky with fog, government buildings stuck with antennas like acupuncture needles.

Neighboring town. Paper mill puking smoke and providing jobs. Marina takes my picture. I just want to take a picture of the mill. I do not smile.

You see. I am learning.

IX.

Logging equipment, factories, bare trees, flat blocks. We sit in the flat of one of the workers. Marina supplies cookies for tea; buys me what I have come to call a cream basket simply because I point them out as my favorite.

Onions dry under the handsome son's bed. The wife has a yellow dress on. They speak quickly. We look at photos, and I sit between Marina, who turns the pages too slowly for my liking, and the father, who is the hunter. The provider. It is a hunting album, for the most part. Antlers on the walls. Tattoos on his hands. I want to sleep. I want her to turn the pages faster. I look over at the soft-spoken man. Sitting beside us, not to show Marina, but to show me. What he loves. I am guilty; I search for common ground, flip back to the cute hunting dogs. He shows me the tags. I ask about the dog competition. He produces a real rabbit foot, six inches, roughly stitched. He caught the rabbit in September. I tell them it means good luck to rub it. He says to keep it. I say thank you, thank you, thank you. I rub it against my cheek. To remember that people love. What they love. People love. To remember. They ate the rabbits and birds he caught. To remember. Two of my favorite Russian songs came on the radio during the car ride home, the snow falling, the sky dark, the flats lighted, the air sharp with cold.

Memory is not fact, a friend says in a letter from Brooklyn. It is perception. What we call the past does not guard fact, it guards reconstruction. Images. Missing. Wishing. Compromises between the involuntary shedding of experience our brains do in spite of us and the light we prefer to cast a history in. Nostalgia: the selection of pleasant memories. Grudges: the selection of unpleasant ones. We are all alone together.

Remember. All the advice that sticks. Remember this, then: love is work. Who we are is different from what we do. Add time and stir if there is no apparent solution.

If you are unsure of a moment's meaning, celebrate the poetry in it. Every act is an act of love. Earth is a hard place to be. Feel thankful for the confusion, because it is yours. We are all alone together.

X.

I work at an old computer in the big meeting room, where I can easily hear the glasses clinking and voices laughing. Teatime. I like knowing the drill. I pour apple yogurt into a black bowl. Vova gives me bread and potatoes for lunch. I am famous for wanting milk in my coffee, which around here is endlessly strange. Sasha looks dashing in his business suit. He is off to give a lecture on forest biodiversity. According to office gossip, his wife rules him. Sugar cubes. Earl Grey. Madonna's latest video, and then the OutKast song about shaking it like a Polaroid picture and lending your neighbor some sugar. I bite into a pastry, groan. I should know by now. Russian food is full of surprises. Ham and cheese inside the chicken. Jam inside the cookie. Fish inside the pastry.

When Ilya asks to look at my passport, he gives me his, and I study every stamp. I point to one. He says My woman. Points to Marina, slim and petite in her green housedress. His marriage registration. I laugh, say Your wife, Ilya. Wife. Marina looks up, smiles, says Woman, maybe other. I am wife. I am almost certain she jokes. Russians often joke about adultery.

Magpies wake me up every morning of third grade because the dog food is kept in a barrel outside my window. Screeches. Yellow beaks. Black and white. I smoke a menthol cigarette outside the tax bureau where Anya waits to have a salary report stamped. It flies between two dingy apartment blocs out of a sunlit morning on my front deck. I bury my head under the rough, pink comforter. I tuck my fingers into my jacket, mint smoke in my mouth, painfully cold air. Can't we just put the dog food somewhere else? Do menthol cigarettes have worse chemicals in them than regular ones?

In the car on the way to the forest, Premslav tries to explain to me the virtue of infidelity. Maybe you are not used to the idea, but when you are young and want to have a family you look for a good father. Later maybe your priority is to have a good lover. I tell him if I cannot find a man who is both I will not marry. Alongside the highway, tan grass and red berry trees. I fix my expression, try to work out the kinks. Learn the Russian glare. Nothing is wrong. My protest, too quick. He studies me, knowing.

XI.

In Syktyvkar, everyone meets at Lenin. In Moscow, Marina informs me, the popular meeting place is Pushkin. There is a statue of him here, too, one

183

arm across his chest, under a stone branch with a nest. He is nicknamed Man Taking A Shower. The three women waiting solemnly for their heroes to come home from the war, a pine branch across their outstretched hands, are Women With Alligator. There is a nickname for every statue. Lenin, the territory of the Komi Republic carved out of the stone behind him, is Man With Backpack.

Against all good judgment my brother watches a video about snakes with Mom. I know better. Still, I am awake in the night. My blankets rustle. I know better than to look. Maybe a man in a trench coat? A mummy. A ghost. Morning, Dan has bags under his eyes, says It was me, I was scared, I tried to get in bed with you. I am nineteen. I turn, lift up the blanket for him, hug him. We sleep. Over and over I turn and lift. He isn't there. Not only that—learn from the statue, the hard gaze of stone. He never was.

XII.

Anya takes me on the majority of her errands. Fresh air. Walk. Tax agency. Her duties as administrator are apparently to answer the phone, type financial reports, and wait in line with them. Wait in line. We wait. In line. She sends me to find cream baskets. I take a ticket, wait in line to buy them, sound out the labels of chocolates and meats. I walk around the block to kill time, still catch myself smiling at old women. They are used to Soviet suspicion; they are caught off-guard by my unlocked expression. I set my face. I am examined quickly. Their features do not change. I begin to teach myself not to look back. One foot. The other foot. A tricky thing to learn. Like tying shoes. Sparse snow. A rifle shop Open 24 Hours. A room filled with tired, long-coated women. Anya is text-messaging Galina on her cell phone. The line has barely moved.

Flat blocks: inevitably gray and trimmed with purple. Flats: identical layouts. Neighborhood: 40,000 people living in cement blocks. Inside a flat: warm. Cooking: something. A family: each member folds up sofa bed in the morning. Stairwell: foul and shadowed. Expression: inevitably solemn and trimmed with suspicion.

XIII.

On the 9th floor of one of the blocks there is a woman with a baby. The woman has a shock of red hair and a deep laugh. The baby is the fifth of her husband's children. His eldest is her age (twenty-nine). She has a little boy with tremendous ears. Like angel wings, she tells me. Which trees are the first to reproduce themselves after a controlled burn? Birch, spruce, then cedar. She makes a mean batch of mayonnaise. When I was fifteen, she says, I led the preteen communist party youth group. I listened to live punk music. I drank beer. I smoked pot. She high-fives her teenage stepson. She explains to me the three generations precipitated by the end of the Soviet era: older than fifty, most can't grasp it. Angry. Thirty-five to fifty, some get it, work new market jobs, some don't and are angry. Under thirty-five, they get it. Oceans away from their grandparents. They have choice. They have selves. They must decide. They must ponder. Better this way, she says. Enough of angry people waiting in lines. She looks with sex at her husband. In ten years they move to the forest, maintain ecological trails, fuck in between the trees. In five more years he takes another woman and leaves her. In fifteen years he gets too old to fuck and she takes two lovers who tell her that her hair is like fire. He leaves her. She leaves him. Three children in the house, none with the same parents. They dance, grab hold, make a family, let go, grab hold of another. Perhaps it is more honest this way. She leaves. He leaves. They dance.

Where are you hiking with that big backpack, Lenin?

XIV.

Summer evening. A girl of five lies with her father in a rough hammock. Oak branches above like dark arms. The air is warm and smells like aging grass. The father pulls the rope, the hammock swings. The girl says Let me do it. She pulls hard. The hammock barely moves. The girl says Let's play Airplane Girl. The father says Okay. Excuse me, miss? Yes, sir? How much time until we reach New York? No, not New York. Where? Um...

185

Seattle. Okay, how much time until we reach Seattle. One hour—what would you like for breakfast, sir? I would like... pancakes. Pancakes? Okay sir, I'll have that coming right up. Would you like juice? No, I would like coffee, and please remember the cream. I always remember the cream! A flight attendant wouldn't say that, sweetie. She would say yes sir, I will remember the cream. The girl leans into her father, smelling baby powder and musk deodorant. They have a secret language, the girl and her father. A cat language. They meow to each other. The daughter says Well then I don't want to be an Airplane Girl.

I am sixteen. I read *1984*. Winston Smith's job has something to do with erasing people from history records. He burns proof, doctors' archives. He aids and abets reconstruction. The enemies of the state were never there.

In the Russia I am living in—and I know by now that it is likely not the one anyone else is living in—a church is replaced by a swimming pool. Later, a church again. I am nineteen and I ask Ilya what the Soviet era was like. His answer, in full: it is over.

The town that bore Lenin's name is now St. Petersburg, as it was before. Russia is not only home to the unscripted touch. Churches and pools do the same dance. Continual editing of the script. Perhaps it is more honest this way. Replacing. Re- forming. It is names, too. They dance.

XV.

I glance at Ilya's purple food. Marina watches, clucking, while I eat soup and meat and cabbage and cake. I want desperately to smoke a cigarette and shower. I do not know the words for Honestly. I just wanted to know what it was. I say Thank you, I'm full. I say Shower. They say Yes. I run into the bathroom, smile. Victory. Marina's voice. My name. Eat. A little bowl, beet shavings in sauce like hay in purple goat diarrhea. For you. Eat. I sit heavily. They laugh. They are my last parents. I swallow tears and beet salad. They have no idea. Inside Russian food there is love.

Sit across from Ilya. Stare straight at the place above his head. He is bent over his studies, a mathematician preparing for a law exam. The world begins. A yellow kitchen, his form, thinking, angular face and large glasses, the red triangle of broad shoulders under his shirt. Breeze lifting curtains. Each morning he sees you at the kitchen door, butters bread, lines salami on top, hands it over without a word. Their wedding album, imposing meaning onto a day no more meaningful than this one. A photo album: a gallop on a circular track. On their wedding day handsome Ilya cannot suppress a smile as they exchange rings. Black and white photos of the traditional walk to a war monument to leave the bouquet. Married during Soviet times. Spectrum of gray. There was still love. A striking picture of Marina, loose dress, flyaway hair, big smile on their Black Sea honeymoon. An instant encapsulates either all meaning or none of it. At what rate? A rate we cannot measure because we live inside it. Ilya's form across the table, the bread and cheese between you. His own saga. Squint. Try to detect his genius in the air, reforming.

XVI.

You are missing the point.

Every love story is not one book, it is two.

Outside my window, the day brightens and darkens with bundled people waiting at a bus stop under tree skeletons. The end is not the plane ride home. Now rain.

The purpose is not a deathbed surrounded by grandchildren. Clouds part.

The apogee is not the wedding day.

Sun, only for nine minutes on the west side of the flat.

I ask my Russian friends about Lenin. Their translations are different: Lenin, the Father of Russian Socialism. Lenin, the Soviet Father. Lenin, the Father of Communism. They speak casually, they care little, they are annoyed by my questions as if they are being asked to dredge up facts from a high school history class.

Lenin, Russian Father. What do you keep in your backpack? A map of your Republic. Seeds.

It is not just the walls that talk. The sidewalks, cracked and wet, tell you that these things never happened. These things you say you remember. Your world never split open every time your father shouted and your mother never devoted herself to painting over the crack. They were never there. We are all alone together. The world splits open against a somber Russian public lot where a couple kisses with passion so palpable it makes your thighs ache.

The window of the plane from Los Angeles, your first polar ice caps, silent, the moon over them.

That moon never happened, either.

There is no broken.

There is only break.

A scar on the heart proves no former wound, it proves only a scar on the heart. Rows of car garages say things in the language of four sides and rust.

They say.

If the past is the purpose then there is no purpose. Someone is breaking into one of the garages.

Past.

Purpose.

Your past purposes.

The purpose of your past.

Birches finger the sky. Over and over again, stand on the asphalt while he drives away, lift the blanket, watch the dark. We are all alone together. Lenin's stare is clear—his eyes are eyeball-less, stone. The world begins. The world begins; it opens out. We quote our aloneness to each other under a gray sky trimmed with purple. We all are calling each other's names back and forth, the sounds arcing through bruised skies like faith long in the gloaming.

Are we alone, all together? Alone, all: we are together.

A forest of birches, fingering. A dark forest.

So dark you can barely see him receding; he is taking decisive steps away from you between cracked white trunks, and finally even his backpack is hidden by branches and leaves.

La Paz and Beni, Bolivia

SICKNESS

July 2012, Rurrenebaque

We all watch her die.

Her eyelids flutter heavily. Her blood trickles to the floor.

First Sylvia looks up from finishing up forms in the pharmacy, her bright fake nails clicking softly. The biochemist Livia, standing beside her, follows her gaze. Laura, the clinic's only nurse, stops on her way out of her office. Roberto the dentist, only here two days of the week anyway, the elusive guy with very dark skin that showcases his truly great teeth, appears and perches on the bench. Antonio, Livia's husband and the resident handyman-plus, grins his usual devil-grin at us as he strides in from the back door.

"Did someone set it up?" Roberto asks.

"Someone had her *killed?*" asks Livia, concern in her soft voice.

"No, she killed herself," says Laura.

"Just now?" asks Doctor Denis, the last to join the group, joining Roberto on the bench. Sylvia nods. The sudsy bathwater has turned red. Wet trails of hair snake below the foam.

"But... *why?*" asks Antonio.

We all turn toward Isaac, a twenty-year-old undergrad from Chapel

Hill here to beef up his pre-med CV. His eyes widen. He balances a worn copy of *Spanish: the Easy Way* on his knee.

"Um," he says.

"*Que pasó*, Isaac?" demands Doctor Denis, who's so young and cheery in his scrubs that he could be the Bolivian Zach Braff. Isaac shadows Doctor Denis most of the time, and Doctor Denis has taken it upon himself to improve Isaac's Spanish.

"I think she—*pienso que...* " Isaac begins, then he turns to me. "It's not just that I don't know the Spanish," he says pleadingly. "There are about ten subplots in this one."

"All *telenovelas* have ten subplots," I answer. "*Isaac no sabe*," I tell Doctor Denis. No one knows, I think, not even the actors. Heads swivel forward again, and I try quietly to capture a photo of the staff staring at the flickering television, since it constitutes that rare moment in which they are all in the same room.

No such luck. The digital clock above the pharmacy flips to 5:00, and each staff member of the Rio Beni Health Project strides confidently off in a different direction, breaking like they'd been huddling for a football play. They each head, however, toward a similar destination: a small house under wide, emerald-green leaves, family, rice, *lomito*, maybe a fried egg on top and some mealy *yucca*.

June 2012, La Paz

For my second trip to Bolivia, seven years after my first, I arrange to stay with Monica for the first week of my time in Bolivia the summer of 2012. The plan is that after a week there with Monica and her husband David in La Paz, I will journey to Rurrenebaque to write more about the Rio Beni Health Project. I met Monica in 2005, when I was staying with a Bolivian writer in La Paz. Then, as now, this time in La Paz comes before changing gears and following the doctors of the Project around in the Amazonian jungle.

Back in 2005 Monica gave me what she called a "Serie de besos:" five photos of her kissing her then-new husband David. I kept one of those photos on my wall for seven years. I hoped to call into my life a romance like that. I wanted to love like they loved.

When I arrive, it's only David who is there. Monica is out of the country at a conference. Perhaps this *cuento* begins when I see him then, seven years after I first meet him, when his wife isn't home. I don't remember his face as much as his demeanor: quiet and gentle. Today, though, he looks perfect. His face stuns me and I'm shy. *Que te sientes en casa*, he says. It's the violet hour outside.

He has good taste in music. The Shins. "Girl Inform Me." I wait for "Caring Is Creepy" but it never plays.

Late 90s-July 2012, Rurrenebaque

This is how Dr. Louis Netzer put it in the late 90s when, on one of his visits home to Santa Barbara County, he spoke to a group of middle schoolers: "About five years ago, I sold my café, and I sold my practice of medicine, and I set out to travel the world. I went to South America and fell in love with Bolivia, so I never made it around the world." When Louis founded the Fundación Salud Rio Beni (the "Rio Beni Health Project" in English) and its clinic, he was not simply—as he would doubtless have put it—on "another adventure." He was also bringing first-time health care to the very poorest people in the very poorest nation in South America.

It's been over a decade since Louis' death from cancer in 2002. Today, his "Bolivian son" Antonio carefully touches up a sign for the Fundación with the familiar red-cross, blue-wing insignia that reads "Fundación Salud Rio Beni: Doctor Louis Netzer" as he stands in the garage behind Louis' legacy: the Rio Beni Health Clinic in Rurrenabaque, the village on the river Beni, the Amazonian tributary where Louis settled instead of continuing to travel the globe. Seatless chairs and power tools litter the unwalled space of the garage, which, structurally speaking, looks more like a tiki hut. A bright yellow bunch of wee bananas hangs to Antonio's left; behind him, a few puppies lie on dried-out palm fronds. Antonio has always been a quiet guy, and I try not to pepper him with questions. He applies his paintbrush and my eyes wander to the puppies. It strikes me that the puppies' flea-ridden fur matches the dusty color of the fronds almost as well as the wings of an electric-blue butterfly matched a pair of silken underwear Antonio and I saw a few days ago in the village of Asunción. Asunción is about one and a half hours upriver (or two, if the boat grounds out and we need to hop out and push against the current, which we did). The underwear was hanging from a stick jutting out of the orange silt riverbank. Antonio was delivering a 200-lb "bio-sand" water filter to a household in Asunción, where about twenty-five families live. I didn't know whether the more surprising sight was the underwear—hanging clothes by the river after washing them in it is routine round these parts, but such a silky fabric is a rarity—or the phenomenal butterfly resting on it. Antonio followed my gaze and chuckled. "It wants salt," he said simply. "If you want to see butterflies, just urinate. After an hour there'll be a lot of them."

June 2012, La Paz

I am exhausted after a long plane flight. David says, sitting at the table with me as I drink the coca leaf tea he gives me for the altitude sickness sure to set in, that he and Monica separated once in the years since I met them. I am flabbergasted. They were so in love when I met them, even if it was seven years ago. What happened? I ask. *I had a crisis*, he says in Spanish, and then, *I don't know why I am telling you this.*

July 2012, Asunción

Lino, a man who looked to be in his early thirties, with sinewy calves and few teeth, appears from between the trees at the top of the bank.

"We've got your filter," says Antonio, gesturing toward the concrete box resting diagonally in the berth, painted bright white with the red-and-blue Fundación insignia stenciled on the side. As he speaks, he stands up from beside the motor and lopes easily down the length of our exceedingly narrow riverboat. Lino and Antonio work together to haul the filter out of the boat, and then Lino does something that surprises even Antonio, who let out a high-pitched giggle: he hefts the filter onto his back and climbs up the slippery bank with it, looking uncannily like a Holy Week participant laboring under the weight of a huge cross.

June 2012, La Paz

After recovering from the initial shock at the idea that Monica and David had spent a period of their marriage separated, my first order of business is to find a local cell phone card. David says it's a holiday so the cell phone place might be closed.

"That's ok," I say after a moment, thick-headed and throbbing with altitude. I sip coca tea. "I realize now that you would be the only person I would think to call."

"*Hermosa*," he says affectionately, embracing me, like *Aaaw*.

1996-1997, Rurrenebaque

The story of the Rio Beni Health Project often begins with a boat crash in 1996, when Antonio was about seventeen. He was already independent from his parents—working, appropriately enough, in Rurrenebaque's Department of Fluvial Transportation—when he saw a skinny, goofy-looking *gringo* struggling to right his boat after driving it into the riverbank. Louis had been attempting to fish, and "didn't realize," Antonio chuckles, "that a river is different than a lake: it has a current."

Amused, Antonio helped Louis back to the property Louis had recently bought, where the skinny doctor was living in a tent. Over coffee Louis confessed that he didn't even know which wood to use to build a cabin. Antonio did, and Louis asked him back at 8 a.m. the next day to work for him. Through daily construction work, the two became close. One day Louis turned to Antonio and said "Come on. We're going to the hospital."

Antonio smiles at the memory. "I didn't really know what was going on, but I went with him anyway," he says. "Louis spoke, well... let's say he spoke his *own* Spanish. I translated for him. I didn't know anything at all about medicine back then."

Louis went to the hospital in nearby Rurrenebaque (or "Rurre") and asked for a room where he could treat the town's poorest patients every Friday for free, with Antonio as translator and general attendant. Locals would also visit Louis in his cabin once word got round, sometimes in canoes they paddled by hand. "It's rare to have someone just show up at a doctor's house, and the doctor react by giving them food no matter what and treating them for free," says Antonio, "but that's what Louis did."

Louis' departure from the California's Santa Ynez Valley—a piece of ranch-ridden wine country between Santa Barbara and San Luis Obispo—had been mourned. He and his wife at the time, had raised their two children in the valley, where Louis had his private practice. He helped found an independent elementary school called The Family School down the road. He brought the tiny town of Los Olivos its first bastion of culture by starting the bohemian Side Street Cafe before the movie *Sideways* put the area's vineyards on the map. He made everyone who came to see him at his office—especially children—feel comfortable. His return from Bolivia was always met with invitations to barbeques at local ranches. After his first trip back home in 1997, Louis returned to Bolivia with an idea for a health foundation for Rurre and its surrounding communities. Its aim would be to amplify and extend what Louis had begun every Friday in that local hospital room: to serve, as Antonio puts it, "those who have absolutely nothing."

June 2012, La Paz

On my second afternoon at Monica and David's apartment in La Paz, Monica is still out of the country. I awaken at 2 p.m. and David sees me and gives me a kiss on the cheek, saying *"Hola California!"* It becomes dark and I still lie on the couch with a headache, brought to my knees by the altitude sickness that travelers joke about because it makes people feel rather stoned: a whole new different kind of being high, ha ha. The Andes nearly touch the stratosphere. David comes with me to take red pastilles from the local pharmacy. *Te faltan globules rojos*, he says. I know it just means my red blood cell count is low, but there's always something more poetic about the way it's phrased in Spanish. *I'm faulted red globes* is what it sounds like to me. A teacher I had in high school once commented that he enjoyed this about Spanish, putting the blame on other things: "In Spanish, you don't drop things," he said, "they fall *from* you."

Late 90s, Rurrenebaque

Louis went on to establish an annual pattern of going home to fundraise and see friends and family from December to March, speaking at venues like the Santa Barbara Library, where he would show slides of the typical jungle maladies in and around Rurre, joking about how excited he was to eat sour cream again. Rotary International quickly sponsored a boat and motor. Back in Bolivia, Louis would stock the boat with various medicines and off he and Antonio would go, Antonio expertly cutting through the morning mist on the river Beni, the boat nosing through the currents, the sleeping boars of mountains furred with jungle launching upward all around.

Because many of the communities served by the Project—which at its height covered hundreds of thousands of square miles of wilderness within the Amazonian jungle bordering Madidi National Park—were unreachable by road, Louis and Antonio often treated people who had never seen a car, let alone met a doctor. Louis' Spanish still left something to be desired, so as the two went door to door, the teenage Antonio quickly learned about diplomacy as he served as Louis' representative in addition to his boat guide. "Is there anyone suffering an ailment here?" Antonio would say. "This man can help with sickness."

June 2012, La Paz

I readily admit that I am taken with David's gentle voice and the way he forms his words. There is something familiar about him that clenches with recognition behind my belly button whenever I sneak a glance at his profile. He checks every time, except this one, if I'd be *molestada* if he smoked.

It comes stilted because I am airsick—though that is of course not what I mean, I mean sick from the lack of air—and the living of it feels as off as trying to tell through a second language. I want to alter the English retelling like it's a translation, since all writing is. There's the living of it, and then the second body, the second skin that doesn't quite fit: into the mother tongue. And then another tongue.

On day two or three of my stay in his apartment, Monica still gone, he arranges a blanket over me as I lie sick with altitude on the couch. Then he kisses me. It's chaste enough, the first time. Not sure when his tongue entered my mouth, large and smooth, a presumptive boat.

"What she doesn't know won't hurt her."

Isn't that what assholes say?

July 2012, Rurrenebaque

Today out back of the clinic, Antonio colors his story about Louis with the high-pitched, drawn out syllables he's taken to using, at some point, to illustrate how everything is and will be okay. *"Al primero, nos escapaban!"* he squeaks: if Louis and Antonio arrived in the evening, community inhabitants, usually of the Tsimani indigenous group, would literally *flee* from the pair of strangers. The pair of interlopers learned to start by visiting with community members in the central part of the village, chatting until late under mosquito nets they brought. The people were curious and shy, friendly and generous. They had all sorts of questions and Lou entertained each of them. Once the people felt comfortable with this square-jawed, slight *loquito* with barely any hair, he would treat them. Once he and his right-hand man made to leave, they'd be asking when the doctor would return.

197

June 2012, La Paz

In David's apartment in La Paz, I get a note from a boy I loved when we were both working in Mongolia. He was a Fulbright photographer there and he broke my heart. He ended it with me because I read his email: one in particular, to a girl I knew he confided in. It was the first time I did something in a relationship I knew I might not be able to justify. In the email I technically had no right to read, he wrote to her that he didn't see a future with me. I cried about what he wrote, and then cried because I'd read it, and confessed; he broke up with me. When I wrote an appreciative letter to him, trying to find the good in the breakup, he responded: "flattery won't get you anywhere with me."

We went silent. He apologized in an email two years later, and two years after that, in 2012, we meet for a drink in DC. I'm at a conference and I've just broken up with a girlfriend who was so clingy and manipulative that I felt deprived of air by the fifth month in. He sees on social media that I'm DC-bound and he lives there, so he reaches out. We get our drink, wander the monuments, and I cry at Lincoln. We have sex within hours. It's been a while since I had a real penis in me and I notice how good it feels. I'm about to leave for Bolivia. We don't decide to be exclusive, especially since I am fresh off the boat from a suffocating and toxic relationship, but we do stay in touch. When I write to him, tapping away at David's living room table, that maybe right and wrong are constructions, he writes something back about poststructuralism. David and Monica's cat statues reside in the corner, frozen in various stretches, orange, polka dotted, on the shelves.

July 2012, Asunción

The afternoon we spend delivering water filters in Asuncion, the person who stands out as the most recently bathed, is Hector. He is one of two teachers at the village's one-room schoolhouse. Antonio, Juan Carlos (Antonio's assistant, whom Antonio affectionately calls "Juanca") and Isaac the intern wrangle a weathered wheelbarrow back and forth, along with a friendly Israeli passing through on a jungle tour who offered to help. Hector the schoolteacher is freshly showered, and orders a quiet and polite 8-year-old girl called Rosario inside her house to fetch a chair for me. He pulls out a cigarette and says in response to my questions that the government sent him here for a three-year term ending in November. "The solitude is the hardest thing," he says, looking me over. "My wife is in Rurrenebaque."

I excuse myself and make my way across the field, where the kids, who get out of school at noon, are playing soccer, and to the cluster of houses shrouded in slightly acrid smoke into which the filter-bearers have disappeared. The fire eats everything, from dried palm leaves to coconut shells in a heap on the ground near the houselets, hens milling nearby. The thin rope stretched between poles a few feet off is not only for clothes; there too hang pieces of an unidentified meat, presumably jerkifying in the late sun. Inside the house, while an adorable toddler paws around in the dirt, an old-before-her-time, missing-toothed, high-cheekboned young mother listens quietly to Antonio giving his spiel: continually fill the new filter with water from the river, he explains. Do that for three days until the water runs *bien clarita,* and then you'll be good to go.

Isaac, dutifully waiting with two white woven sacks, opens them and pours two scoops of gravel and several of sand into the filter on top of a metal plate resting inside. After the water is poured atop that sand, usually by the heftiest family member around, he fits another metal plate over the top of the filter as a lid. When we bring the filter to Lino's house—or when Lino brings it, all alone on his back—his family (or friends) crouch nearby outside a pitched tent that now serves as a permanent residence. "So the microbes don't get in," Lino says proudly, watching Isaac fit the lid to the body of the filter as several children play at karate chops behind him. Nearby, a boy in a yellow T shirt absently scratches his shin, then does so a second later, then again. Antonio, as usual, catches me looking. "Leishmaniasis," he says softly to me.

Out here, it's a damning diagnosis. As with many afflictions of the poorest Bolivians, the Leishmanaisis parasite is treatable, but the access to timely health care from a place like this jungle and the knowledge of when it's necessary to do so run scarce. Leishmanaisis begins with a mosquito bite that itches more than should be humanly possible, and opens after a few weeks into a wound. Leishmanaiasis figures among the more prominent health problems in *"las comunidades"*, which technically means simply "the communities," but which is project shorthand for "rural areas deep in poverty and often just as deep in the jungle." Back at the clinic, Doctor Denis shows me photos on his cell phone: a flesh-eating bacteria that leaves crumbling holes where noses have been, a bit like Ralph Fiennes' Voldemort in the *Harry Potter* film franchise. The poster in Laura's nurse's office features a snapshot of an afflicted mouth, which was too nightmarish for words because it wasn't really a mouth anymore. Doctor Denis recently snapped a photo of an afflicted buttock, with an open, weeping wound the size of a saucer.

I look at the boy near Lino's tent, a boy with gorgeous long eyelashes, and am unable to stop myself glancing at a mosquito supping on my forearm. "I've had Leishmaniasis twice," Antonio says to me when he sees my horror. "Two years ago, I had it. It's only really bad when it goes untreated, when the wound opens and opens and weeps and weeps. And when they don't get treatment. Or don't finish treatment."

The treatment for Leishmaniasis calls for huge injections in the rear, daily for twenty days, with dosage varying according to the patient's weight, ramping up the amount of Glucantime, a substance that looks like water and comes in a tiny vial. The nurse Laura handed me one of the vials once. It looked like that which might contain an upscale anti-wrinkle serum of the sort one finds in duty-free cosmetics shops in cosmopolitan airports. It was made in France.

June 2012, La Paz

David takes me to a lookout famous in La Paz. We watch the sunset bathe the uncanny mountains red. I cannot believe how familiar he is, like a molasses-slow reverberation from another life. I feel almost sick with recognition. I think you could be the love of my life, he says in Spanish. It's crazy. I know what he means.

It's my third or fourth day in La Paz. The objects around me, the ones I brought in my large square bag, become characters as I fasten onto them: face wash with microbes in it from a drugstore that I bought because it was light enough to get through security. A long sweater that ties at the waist from a thrift store. I feel vaguely that the apartment is swirling slowly around me, as though I'm in a structure that spins slightly faster than the thousand-miles-per-hour at which earth and all of its inhabitants spin. I don't know if this is because of the altitude sickness or because David steps naked into the shower with me after that first tongue kiss, and the groping on the lookout.

If I asked him to leave and then left myself, I would eventually need to tell Monica why I didn't feel comfortable staying in her house. So instead I make a decision. I am conscious about making a bad decision consciously. Or, making one that feels out of step with what I've generally thought to be my moral code. Most of my close friends and most of my mentors have carried on something with someone taken, or with someone while they were taken. Bad things don't seem to befall them, and they have always been good to me. They've had affairs and I don't think they're bad people. I am exhausted by the thought of trying to keep a man at bay who wants me when I want him so badly that my oxygen-thinned body throbs. I can barely climb the stairs without my heart hammering. How am I supposed to tell my host "no" when he covers me with a blanket and kisses me? What on earth am I trying to prove? I am not writing so much as letting the rhythm of the throbs dictate what I say: something has made a monster of me.

July 2012, Rurrenebaque

"This is part of why I have become most interested in capacity-building," Antonio says, bringing me back to the present in the garage as he dots a red "I" on the clinic sign with his paintbrush. "Even when we get the right medicines to a family with three kids who are all sick with something different, sometimes the parents can't read the instructions. And that's where the cycle breaks. That's where we have to work and improve." As with the tuberculosis Tracy Kidder describes making inroads into Lima,

Peru, and Russia in *Mountains Beyond Mountains,* the terrifying reality is that while treatment for Leishmaniasis is officially free in Bolivia, all too many of the worst cases of Leishmaniasis afflict those who can't access treatment or who don't quite follow the instructed days and doses of the medicine. When the Leishmaniasis reappears after an unfinished course of treatment, it's stronger and more resistant. And, like various maladies in hard-up countries, free government treatment for it is just the beginning. Schoolhouses like the one presided over by Jon the comely teacher, and the ever-scarce boat motor fuel for anyone who'd like to get to town from the communities or get to a doctor in communities *from* town, are as vital to detection, treatment, and recovery as the prized medicine itself.

June 2012, La Paz

It happens twice. First it's on the floor of the living room. David keeps saying my name. I ask him to come down to where I lie because the skin-to-skin contact gets me off. I'm used to this being an unusual request; with both men and women, it's missionary that sends me to the moon and rough sex that makes me too sore to come. I have long worried this makes me vanilla and boring.

David doesn't really come down when I ask him to, but then asks me to tell him what I like. I'd like you to come close, I say again, and mumble something in Spanish about contact and skin. When he finally does lower himself and I cry out, he says *I like it when you shout.*

Outside it is darkening, violet; past the point where half the buildings were caught up in sun, past when the buildings fall dark and the sun only hits the uncanny, monstrous mountains behind them.

July 2012, Rurrenebaque

From Direct Relief, to Concern, America, to Nezter-Brady International, the Rio Beni Health Project has had many "parent" organizations, but it's always had the same "uncle:" Chris Brady, whose surname now appears alongside Netzer's in the Clinic's parent organization and whose own kids attend the country school Louis helped found in Los Olivos. "I just go nuts if I can't be working with disadvantaged people," Chris once said to me, nearly physically keening out of his lawn chair during one of my many visits to his house in Los Olivos.

He was digressing. In reality, it takes many visits to get a whole, straight story out of the guy. "Ebullient" is the only word for Chris, and his intentions are as good as his brain was scattered whenever I tried to gather information from him in his flowered backyard. Educated in Development Studies at Berkeley in the eighties, with decades of experience on multiple continents and three cases of malaria under his belt, Chris is one of those veteran development workers who hungers palpably for the kind of work done out in the Bolivian Amazon. He's also the only other person in the Santa Ynez Valley with the same crackling energy as Louis Netzer himself had, and the same fearless attitude toward blazing trails. Chris and his brother Jim organized annual bike and trekking trips for local Santa Barbara high school students to visit the clinic every summer for the better part of a decade, and it is Christopher's furious work on behalf of the clinic's staff that kept the Project from closing completely in 2010, when it seemed inevitable that the clinic would close its carved wooden doors for good.

"When *was* the economic crisis in America?" Joselo Hurtado, the Project's executive director and administrator, rubs his cheek one sunny afternoon in his office in Rurre, where first-time-patients at the clinic met with him. Joselo, a handsome fellow with salt-and-pepper hair, talks as rapidly in Spanish as Chris Brady does in English, which is saying something. "Must have been 2009, no?" he mutters. "Because in 2010 the crisis reached us."

That was the year it looked like the jig was up. Charismatic Louis, with his loyal following of old patient families in the Santa Ynez Valley and his adorable stutter, wasn't there anymore to drum up enthusiasm. The team often had to wait to be paid while Chris scrambled and advocated in every direction he could think of for the funds to pay their salaries. Gone are the days of spending half the working week in the communities, training young *promotores* in community health work and doling out anti-parasites to schoolchildren—all of which I saw firsthand when I visited the Project in 2005.

August 2005, Rurrenebaque

I am twenty, in Rurrenebaque for the first time to write about the Rio Beni Health Project. I meet Medi, a mop haired handsome of the Bolivian variety. I think we are the same age; I am twenty, but still, it's the first time I feel a peer's youth: he's clumsy and what my big sister calls "rabbit-y" and the jackhammer way we're fucking hurts and I ask him to stop and he whines that he is horny and asks me to go down on him, which I don't, on some sort of principle. I don't remember how we met, but I'm guessing it's because his father is one of the chefs at my favorite little restaurant in town. I don't remember whether the room we have sex in is a hotel or a hostel or a house. I think we go swimming together in sharp sunlight. There is one foreigner hangout where I learn from Israelis about their army requirement and eat chocolate cake at the bar, talking with the Australian owner, when Medi doesn't come looking for me after that night. I interview the mayor, Yerko, who is young, early thirties at most, and he explains the different forces at work around the health project, and he looks tired and I say in Spanish something along the lines of, it must be hard to try and make it all work, and he says heavily that it is and we should finish up over dinner. Later I will repeat what all we drank to Chris back in California: apparently one bottle of wine is customary and I shouldn't have expected anything then, but the second is when it veers into murky waters. The restaurant has a parrot, I think, and is attached to a hotel, and Yerko is upset when he hears I swam in the river with some other hostel people I don't remember well, probably my Israeli buddies. Yerko says I undermined his authority and I tell him *I told you something as a person but you responded like a mayor* and he says I am right. Then I convince him to donate gasoline to the health project for the boats they take to the farthest communities that are not reachable over land. He calls me niña hermosa and I have tried since then to remember when our first kiss is, exactly, but I know he gets a key to a room and that he is hard and rubs against me and I like it but also say I want to go home, and when he flies over the cobblestones with me holding him on his motorbike, I say what about *los autoridades*, meaning police, and he responds, "*Yo soy la autoridad.*" I am *the authority*.

And in the humid air amid the deep green that crowded in jungle tones around the borders of the polished cabana restaurant where we ate, where the attending man would clearly keep the secret of the room and our presence there, I ask on the motorbike if he has siblings and he says only sisters and I say so you are the *hijo mimado*, the special spoiled one that a person is if they are the only girl or only boy, and he says heavily that yes he is, and I lean into his back and he tips his head back, and then I am back at my hostel and the next day I am having lunch with a girl who works for the project and he approaches and confirms his donation, and Joselo the on-location team manager in Bolivia writes me a thank you email saying I was in his head last night and I must have bewitched him with my eyes and it is not until I speak with Chris, the project head in California that I hear Yerko has a wife and child, and that I was lucky nothing else happened, it could have been worse, and the gasoline does not show up, not for years, but by 2011 apparently Yerko has become *simpatico* to the cause and a good man to work with, says Chris the team manager in California who gives me a longish peck on the lips when I leave his house the way my mother and father peck their friends on the lips at the end of their book club.

June 2012, La Paz

The story of how they first fucked: Monica told me seven years ago. David tells me now. It's actually the only thing they each tell, independently of one another, more or less the same way: it was fantastic. It was huge.

David was technically dating Monica's cousin at the time, so it was kind of a mess.

But "*tremendo—y bueno*" is how he describes it to me. He had to go to work and could not wrap his head around what had just occurred, falling drunkenly into bed with Monica. He just knew it was tremendous, and good.

August 2005, Rurrenebaque

In 2005 the Project has much more funding than it will later from Direct Relief International, but ironically, with the exception of Antonio and Joselo, not only is the Project team peopled with different folks back then, but a more interpersonally dysfunctional group of people would be hard to find. A twenty-year-old as untrained in journalistic standards as I am in the ways of the world, I am afraid to write anything other than straight-up P.R. about what I see happening. I mention several times in the article I write about Joselo's frequent use of the phrase "we're a team" in Project team meetings, as a reason to believe in the unity of the clinic staff. In reality, it is Joselo trying desperately to encourage coherence in a group of people who are professionally and personally terrible matches for each other. *Telenovelas* couldn't make this stuff up. Doctora Andrea, an overbearing woman who cries at nearly every team meeting, sets the teeth of the visiting American doctor and his wife on edge. The marriage of those Americans is on the rocks, and one of the doctors is sleeping around on his wife with Vero, the daughter of Paula, a team nurse. The American doctors (there used to be a rotation of them, but the money to fund that arm of the Project dried up) conspire to bring Vero with them to the States. Paula feels personally affronted when Joselo, who has just come on board to clean things up as the new manager, starts asking her for pharmacy records. ("You don't trust my *word?*" she gasps when Paulo asks her to use pen and not pencil.) The American doctor's wife plans her route home carefully so as to avoid the town gossips, who happen to include Paula, and Andrea. Andrea is married to Humberto, a much older sociologist who knows a great deal about Bolivia's tragic and socialist-friendly history and keeps the most sparse and unhelpful patient registration forms Joselo has ever seen. Antonio even adds to the drama by virtue of having impregnated one of the American volunteer doctors during a long relationship with her. (The mother and baby have lived, since midway through the pregnancy, in America. Antonio's first daughter is now twelve, and he'll meet her in person for the first time in 2012.)

June 2012, La Paz

David is out. I chat online about my moral dilemma with a gay male friend who is doing human rights work in Nicaragua. My friend has had multiple dalliances with married men, but the men are married to women and the country in which these interludes occur has a high level of homophobia. I think this gives me him more of an excuse, if an excuse is called for.

My friend asks me to describe David. It's like he walked out of my high school crush dream machine, like he is my own personal Adonis, I write. His face, his mop of dark hair, his round spectacles. Like Gael García Bernal, with Lennon glasses.

It's his *job* if he looks like that, comes my handsome gay friend's reply.

July 2012, Rurrenebaque

Given the problematic team dynamic, it's understandable how an official letter sent around 2010 to one of the Project's German donors detailing alleged "mismanagement" of Project funding would have unsettled Christopher back in the states. In his office today, I can nearly see Joselo's clear features grow more lined as he remembers that period, and his flecked hair grow whiter as he makes a face of exhaustion and disgust. "Someone had gotten information they could only have gotten from *here,* in my office," he says, gesturing to the shelves of binders and files behind him. "I would have been happy to supply anything to anyone, it's just that whoever it was didn't have the guts to say it to my face."

He suspects either Humberto or Andrea whose *despedidas* from the Project were at the outset amicable ones. The Project couldn't pay them what they'd been earning, and Bolivian law prohibited adjusting their contracts so they earned less. Andrea had left even earlier; in spite of the fact that the young community health *promotores* she'd trained were to serve their communities without payment, she herself wasn't willing to try to "live on patience." "Patience won't *feed* us," she retorted when Chris tried, on his annual visit, to level with the team about the gravity of the Project's predicament.

At the memory of the German letter clusterfuck, Antonio, touching up the sign, grins. Antonio's grin is his general response when faced with difficulty. "Someone even started a rumor that when Chris came down here *I'd* get him drugs and women," he chuckles. "Humberto and Andrea thought the rest of the team had something against them—when really, even though Humberto in particular wasn't doing much, they still were paid more than everyone. The rest of us worked overtime on boats on the weekends to be ready to leave for Mondays, just working without pay so everything would go okay. Humberto planted some seeds—seeds of rumors. We had to get Chris down here to do damage control. He listened in on a call I made to Humberto, asking him why he'd said all that stuff. So Chris knew that's how the rumor had started, but he was still pretty pissed off."

"Did you see Humberto after that?" I ask.

"Not much. Andrea got cancer and went for treatment. She and Humberto separated, then got back together. They live in another town. I actually did see him just the other day, though."

"How did it go?" I ask, expecting a story of a showdown.

"Just *fine*," Antonio says with that upward lilt that gives humor to his words. "He's old now, and fragile. He's just a little bit of a *nut*case. That's what we all decided when the board audited Joselo after that letter, and found absolutely nothing wrong. Just a *viejito loquito*. I mean, what are you going to do?"

August 2005, San Miguel

Humberto's slim form disappears in front of me between cane stalks on a trip out to the rural indigenous community of San Miguel. His disembodied voice floats out from between sun-drenched stalks: "It's the social aspect that's the most important. That the young people learn more." He then emerges with a few choice stalks and hands one to me before disappearing to conduct another session with schoolchildren about hand washing.

I don't see Humberto again until it was time to return to the boats at the end of the day. "What do you like most in life?" he asks me just as we enter the shady part of the path and a light breeze cradles our bones and cools off our sweat. The answer is simple on a day like this one. "This moment, for example," I tell him. "I'm not in pain, I'm content, in a beautiful place with someone interesting and intelligent to talk to. I am believing more and more that heaven is something we get now, in the good moments. And you?"

"The same," he answers. "People who are interesting and intelligent and sensitive to have discussions with. One cannot allow problems to be what one thinks about. I have had some big problems, some serious problems. One has to be where one is and think about the good."

We are quiet for a time, and I twirl the large almond tree leaf that Humberto left on my purse at lunch. He likes to leave gifts for people. He likes to play tricks.

July 2012, La Paz

Monica's grandfather dies, while I am there and Monica is away. David goes to cut his wife's grandfather's nails, help carry his corpse down the stairs. He is morose when he returns to the apartment. I wonder how his wife would comfort him. I wonder if trying to comfort him is the right thing to do, or if it somehow serves a selfish desire to be a certain kind of woman to him. The wife is the one who should be there, doing that. The wife is the one I came to see. I have allowed something to happen that would hurt her.

More than that. I sucked his dick. It wasn't my best performance; I lack much practice with uncircumcised *penes*. After a few drinks he feels less sad about his grandfather-in-law. I missed you, he says to me—he brightens after I make him laugh. "Don't Stop Til I Come" by Brazilian Girls comes on; he put it in the CD rotation. It's a remix I haven't heard.

August 2005, San Miguel

"That anteater cuddled into your arms, didn´t it?" Humberto says suddenly.

It had. It was just a baby. This morning on the lunch-food stockpiling stop, a barefoot family of many children and a mother whose face had grown lined before its time waited to see whether I would buy the anteater. The children had been mishandling it, as happened with most animals around here and which upset me the same way I am more upset by the prospect of stunt-double horses falling down in movies than stunt-double people doing so. Humberto had gone to look at the baby anteater then waved me over to take a picture. When the mother placed the anteater in my arms it cuddled and leaned its long nose over my arm. I stroked it and said, "Hi little one," and wished I could somehow take it to my home in California and let it go free. Here either someone will buy it and kill it for its pelt or these children will kill it inadvertently. Barefoot and hungry, the children got no such attention from me, and now my guilt about that reaction is heavy. I say as much to Humberto, who nods gravely.

Humberto knew and worked with guerrilla folks in the jungle. At least, that's what someone murmured to me once. Humberto doesn't speak of anything like that directly, but tells me more than once that he still needs to "*tender cuidado*," to constantly be aware of who might want to harm him. We don't speak of the reason for such caution. Humberto enjoys talking about animals instead.

June 2012, La Paz

Monica returns to La Paz on my fifth day but goes to her family's home for the night because of her grandfather. After two beers and cigarettes, alone unexpectedly since Monica chose to sleep at her grandmother's, we laugh hard. I have a fever. He puts a thermometer in my mouth after rubbing a cotton ball on it that I guess had alcohol on it. We kiss around the thermometer. The moment is bathed in warm, tinted light for me and I don't know why. My pink shirt? He looks at me washing dishes and says, you're even lovelier, what happened to you?

Who knows. That I'm sick, my cheeks are flushed. That his wife draws ever closer.

What happened to me?

August 2005, San Miguel

"I imagine that if I were a hen, I would like sugarcane juice on a day like this," I say to Humberto as we walked back to the town's thatch-roofed *cede social de la comunidad,* where the doctors are packing the bags for reloading onto the boats.

"If you were a hen, would you be happy?" asks Humberto. We laugh.

"We have no way to know that," I say. "All we see and feel and know, we see and feel and know through the filter of being *seres humanos.*"

Humberto and I rail at the limits of our human knowledge on the boat ride back to Rurre. What could it be like to be a mayfly with a 24 hour life span? Or a planet, with one of millions of years? We are doing what we do from inside ourselves, within the limits of our eyed and mortaled situation among the rocks and bugs. We can't lift ourselves out of it. I think of that afternoon, and the white imprints left by the sugar cane on the large wooden cylinders that smush the cane into cracking and dripping juice, the cylinders made to turn by the long log, Humberto and me laughing, pushing it in a wide circle.

July 2012, Rurrenebaque

"What about those trips, to schools?" I ask Antonio in the garage, shaking myself out of the reverie. "And the promotor program?"

Promotores were brought to Rurre and educated in health issues, designated as first responders, and they took pledges in front of their home communities to stay there and serve.

"We still have about five *promotores,*" Antonio says, dipping the brush now into the red paint. Andrea's not here to teach new ones, though, and we can't pay to bring them in or get out there ourselves."

The clinic's current staff is entirely made up of twentysomethings now, with the exception of thirty-four-year-old Antonio, who was nineteen when Louis sent him for two years to a nursing program and who has since also trained as a lab technician, an auto mechanic, and community capacity-builder. Many things occur to an observer after learning of the depth and nature of Louis's relationship with Antonio. One is the parallel universe in which Antonio never met Louis. This-life Antonio met his wife in a hospital during a capacitation course, after all. There would be no Livia married to Antonio. There would perhaps be no Louis for as long as there had, because Louis might have crashed his boat at some other, more nefariously-weathered time. Antonio's family history is not a subject of public discussion, but by the time he met Louis at seventeen, he was financially independent from his family. In a small town in the middle of rural South America, this is not the usual case for teenage boys. When Louis was diagnosed with terminal pancreatic cancer and given a few months to live, he returned to Rurre to tie up loose ends—the most important of which was seeing Antonio one last time.

June 2012, La Paz

David talks to Monica across the table, toward where she sits behind me, working on a philosophical essay about hermeneutics (if I've understood correctly). "Naked As We Came" comes on a few minutes after she gets up to go sleep, still in the purple jacket I tell her looks very hip. I go to the kitchen to clean up after dinner and he follows me, kisses me hard in the dark, his hand comes down my pants, my hand goes down his, we free the clothing, he enters me on my tippy toes, my back arched against the kitchen counter. "*Quieres estar solos con migo*" he asks as we move—I say yes—he says "me too, *muy solos*"—I'm crinkling the paper of the baguette I bought them for dinner with my hands, afraid out the corner of my eye she'd be standing there—

July 2012, Asunción

Only at the last minute does Antonio stand at the river's edge in Asunción, waiting for payment from the family with the boy who's scratching his sores. A filter is seventy *Bolivianos:* about twelve US dollars. Several adults come out to meet him there, including a *chola* I hadn't seen before—a round-bodied grandmother, with two long braids of silver hair. Between them all, Antonio is satisfied with what he's given. Then they pass him a large stalk of plantains, long and green. Antonio grins and skids down-bank, laying the cluster in the boat alongside a brown hen nestled under the prow. The hen's quiet manner startles me as much as the norm of cheerfulness I see among the adults in Bolivia, especially the men. I'm similarly startled by how quiet the children are, too young to have children and too old to cry. The hen's feet are tied, and every time she tries to move she ends up face down in the sandy boat. She was a gift from another family, earlier in the day.

The river moves smooth as glass until Antonio starts the motor. The quieter moments like these are easy to lose to feeling hopeless, even given the fact that the filters are a life raft serving children like the little girl I see waving from the banks of the Rio Beni as the engine cranks to life. I watched her mother wash clothes from the cliffs above the river, which sounded its low hum always, and struck me as a worthy thing to pray to daily. Such a swirling, eddying constant could surely carry away one's doubts for a small while. The girl waves again. I wave back. Access to those other things that prevent health disasters, primarily education, isn't likely to appear in her life before her children do. A drizzle begins to pock-mark the surface of the river, peppering the engine-wrinkled surface of the water.

June 2012, La Paz

Perhaps, since the sex is fairly predictable, from a narrative point of view, this is simply a story of how I surprise my*self.* Yerko I genuinely didn't know had a family. David I know does. Perhaps this is a tired yarn about how I joined the ranks of people who do bad things, or at least hurtful things, knowingly—or people who see that it's murkier than that. David describes marriage as *una relacion formal. Una relacion reconizado por el estado.* When he is drunk he tells me how Monica told him she wanted a baby. "Ok, you want to have a baby with ME? No, she doesn't say that. Just that she wants a baby," he said.

Monica walks me to what she calls the blueberry cafe. She orders, and *de repente,* I think of how he'd show off my younger body in front of his friends if he left her for me.

I had so been looking forward to staying with my friend and her husband. Where do these thoughts come from? Who is the person having them? There's something capitalist about sexuality, the heteronormative marriage kind, especially when the Other Woman stuff comes into play. Something about performing for a man a certain function, a service.

David says that when she left for the conference, she told him to behave himself.

July 2012, Rurrenebaque

When we arrive back in Rurre and unload, I walk back to the hostel by way of the riverbank. Among the warm wood, the soft mud covered with bodies of trees as far as the eye can see, specked with petals, little slits of red like small wounds.

June 2012, La Paz

"I told her I had something to tell her," David says to me, "but that before I did, she should know I'll be with her."

We were standing in the laundry room and I had to ask him to repeat himself. He was talking about breaking the news that her grandfather had died while she was away.

July 2012, Rurrenebaque

Here, today, in Rurre: Antonio's son with Livia, who is five, waits for his father to finish unloading. His ears are noticeable, like little wings on his head. His name is Louis.

June 2012, La Paz

He says, sitting at the table, "I don't know if it's more difficult to be in your place or mine."

"When you go, I'll cry," he says. "That's all."

July 2012, Rurrenebaque

Birds have begun to fly south and they astonish me every time they glide overhead. It was through Lou, handing a lovely piece of short writing explaining his need to go adventuring to my mother during our last family checkup with him, that I learned the meaning of the phrase "swan song." That day Louis checked me for diabetes. I was eight. He made me giggle by allowing the screen door to shut behind him before informing me soberly, "You're normal."

July 2012, La Paz

I leave without telling either of them. I can hear them arguing at 4 a.m. and I can feel the sickness rising, as though my blood has turned black. I am not a good force in their home. I should go. I'm like a walking malady.

I take a small bag to Rurre on the "Most Dangerous Road in the World." The trip takes thirty-six hours; it is supposed to take eighteen. I travel with a bunch of Bolivians and some chickens. The *chola* next to me greets me formally when she first sits down next to me. *Que llegemos,* she says to me. A prayer that we arrive. Across the aisle from us, a cheery potbellied fellow drinks the first of several cans of beer: to *Diosito*, that we arrive safely. We get stuck in the orange mud for six hours and arrive in Rurre at dawn. Under my feet is my small bag. I leave my big square bag there, in Monica and David's apartment.

The big square bag becomes a point of contention because after I have a change of heart during a period of intense water-borne sickness in Rurrenbaque. The owner of the hostel comes to check on me when I don't get up well into the afternoon. My bones hurt, and I decide to send Monica a letter from Rurrenebaque with the truth and my apology. Monica and David put my bag into the street. That's what they tell me they have done, anyway, shortly before I stop hearing from either of them. My long sweater, a necklace belonging to my grandmother, and a few other favorite things are in there.

Back in La Paz, I visit the guard's room of their apartment building before leaving Bolivia. The guard is sure they wouldn't have put the bag out.

"It's a foolproof plan," the guard comments.

"What?" I say.

"Just say that they got rid of your things, and sell them. I wonder how many young women they've done this to."

I feel anger then, that I may not have been the only one. That they have something of a marital-drama racket going on. Monica comes from wealth, but doesn't like accepting money.

A new friend I have made in La Paz as I wandered the streets aimlessly for the day between flights accompanies me to the apartment. Monica is out. I want to check the apartment for my bag. David is there. We are both shaking. The bag isn't anywhere I can find. There's something sort of comical about it. He tries to tell me it's gone: I say I know, but just to be sure.

This has all caused us both a lot of damage, he says.

I know not to be surprised at that, at the way his choice of words helps his cause as the done-to. Suddenly what happened, happened *to* him. It damaged him like it damaged her. It's my job now to fall from them. There are bags half-filled with his stuff, but I'd bet money she let him back in after a suitable period of angry weeks.

I remember how he abandoned all the things he said, love of my life, and whatnot, and the hurt and self-righteousness festers like a sore. I write once more, and ask them please to understand that there was jewelry in that bag, and that I hadn't wanted to start a war with Monica but rather admit my mistake because she deserved to know what happened in her house. The last thing that happens from anyone to anyone is a transaction: David sends my mother $100 through moneygram that Fall, to pay for the necklace of her mother's that I lost because I fucked the husband of the couple in the house where then I left my bag.

I can't blame the altitude for this stupidity. Stupidity isn't a sickness, and it was all a transaction.

"Mistress 101," jokes a friend: "when you leave, make sure you're all the way gone."

July 2012, Rurrenebaque

Louis wrote an "open letter" when he got sick about being on the beach and watching his love walk along the water. His love was not the wife he had children with, or the artist he had an affair with. His love was the French mother of his daughter's husband.

In his letter goodbye, Lou wrote that he was bundled up against the sea wind while his love picked up rocks or shells. "I renew my pact with G-d," he wrote.

The river is quiet now. I stand not rooted to the spot but rooted, water leaning into the dark tongue of the wind, mounds of mountain like sleeping boars. It is this river that Lou glided on top of in a boat, this river the people pray to, this river that was part of his decision to stay. The image he gave when he used to tell us about it on his trips back to Santa Barbara made such a powerful imprint that it tugs at my throat now with a recognition so strong it is almost painful, the wind warm and humid, the evening soft and natural as a moth against my lips.

"How do you renew your pact with G-d, Louis?" I ask here at the river's edge on my last night in Rurrenebaque, after weeks observing the health project whose existence is owed to him. At that moment another V of birds flies low over the calm water, close by and nearly gliding on its surface, and for a fleeting moment I understand that here in the fresh evening the birds are doing just that, that I am doing just that by watching them, that that is all any of us ever do.

It's all for love. Those were the last words he uttered before dying, I have heard, uttered to the lover and children at his bedside. I walk away from the river by the light of a waxing moon, light ricocheted off its surface from a bright star opposite, a bright star I cannot see to affirm its existence but that must exist, and I trip on the uneven bank, and as I walk past someone's yard, where coal burns, glowing in a little stove, I hope that in some way it is all any of us ever say.

California, USA

COYOTE

—

Out the open barn door there was a tree, standing against the baking sky in sharp outline. It was an oak, normal for this area, but a taller one, a more up-reaching one, a slenderer one than most. Near the end of the Aikido lesson a flake of moon, light as something one is forgetting, appeared off to its left, sky still roused with afternoon, and it reached.

I always have trouble getting to sleep. I finally put myself to sleep the other night by recalling how it felt to be thrown, the rich flop of a *gi* on the mat. I conjured the particular feel of each classmate's hand around my wrists. Betty (expert), Anne (gentle), Jenny (unsure), Cassie (wide), Nate (questioning), Matt (ouch). Incense, spearmint-green mats, Tautahcho standing erect off to the side in his black *hakama* calling out one through ten in Japanese as we hurled ourselves downward only to spring up again, panting, belts and braids coming loose.

I saw the tree during the two years the Muhu Dojo was in the barn when we stretched our upper backs, peeking through the window made by my left arm as I reached my right arm under it.

More than once I have put myself to sleep by closing my eyes and flying back to the mountain, stars winking, red dirt, sagebrush.

My father would wait for me at the end of class. Often he had gone for coffee and a library hour or two. Often he had bought a cold tea drink for me. We listened to the radio and raced to call out the name of the artist and song. Whoever won earned five points, but we never kept track.

Since my school is on the way into town from the mountain, some days Tautahcho, or "T," or "Tauch," brought me to Aikido. One day I ran out to the parking lot to see his old red truck receding. I ran tearfully over to the elementary school across the creek to see whether any parents were late in ferrying their offspring into the valley. I found Tara, one of the only other Chumash visible to the white colonizer and settler community I'm part of, and an adopted relative of T. She wasn't planning to leave quite so soon, but she gave me a ride.

Orange of old leaves emerging shyly in dawn. Fog along mountains, light spreading bands of seashell pink, branch and wildlife stirring. But before: night. A blank page. Coyote's bright eyes meet with mine, maybe twelve inches between us, and a pane of glass, glass which will blow out in a matter of seconds. Many sounds: singing, screeching, screaming.

It could be earmarked as misplaced affection.

—

When Betty's dad died, he left her with just enough to buy a piece of heaven way, way up road a ways outside of the small towns clustered north of Santa Barbara. Betty and T and their son, Levi, and half the time Betty's two older children, Cassie and Sam, lived in canvas tents up there during the year they were building the cob house. I stayed overnight once that first year, and the wind was so hot and the canvas so loud when it flapped that I did not sleep but sat, hugging my legs on the makeshift deck, smelling sage, feeling heat on my skin in starlight so strong I could read leaves on the pepper tree. The canvas flapped all night long.

I went to a boarding school described as a "hippie commune" by New York friends who hear me tell of it, but my parents lived close enough to give me a lift to Aikido three times a week. The good times in the car make me grateful for this, either insightful talks about politics with Mom or goofy chats about words with Dad. The other times I spent Aikido class recovering from my father's latest rage attack. One of these times Tautahcho stopped supervising locks and throws long enough to do work on my back, digging into pressure points. I felt darkness ooze into the pink slabs of muscle and then sink around the place T touched, the muscles contracting so that they could then relax. I sobbed. One of these times T said only this, in a kind and quiet voice: "Ming just needs to be nurtured."

I stayed for a few days here and there on the mountain one summer. When I would wake up early enough on the mountain, I joined T, Betty and whoever else was passing through for the sunrise ceremony in which we sang. We blessed each other with smoke from burning sage and asked the mountain's spirit for the protection and well-being of our loved ones. When they said they would think of me while I was in rural Russia, what that meant was T asking during sunrise, "Please take care of her" while I was gone.

Muhu means "owl" in Chumash. Tautahcho's last name is Muhuawit. The nonprofit office I worked for while away had the owl as its mascot. I went on to bring T back owls made of wood I found in marketplaces in Ecuador, drew him one for Christmas. He gave me a journal, blue with pagodas embroidered on it.

One day when back on the mountain, I filled in a trench, reddish dirt raining onto long white pipe. I stopped with coarse shovel in hand to watch sky appear in fleeting patches. A cat rubbed my legs, and I picked her up. She kneaded into my shoulders, purring and smelling dusty. I was re-familiarizing myself with the nature of dirt after my first year not at a ranch school, breaking clods with the dull blade of the shovel edge, tossing powder into the ditch where it ran down sides of pipe like water, scraping gravel level. I was glad Tautahcho wasn't around today to see my body awkward, fledgling, and soft-handed once more, struggling with more dust than Eliot's puny handful. Fingers used to typing, feet to sidewalk.

Levi staged his own graduation ceremony recognizing completion of a repeated year of first grade, and his parents played along. Betty drew a poster for him. But it's T who bought the party poppers from Longs Drugs and strawberry pie with card saying *Congratulations to my baby boy, Love dad*, and looked through his son's scrapbook from the year, stopped at the new year's resolution to read better, "And you do," the spry old man said, hugging the child on his lap, clearly glad.

Betty and Leann and I go for a walk after supper among thistles and thin air swelling with heat, earth covered in sprawling brambles and fluttering insects and heady sage. Animals aren't babies anymore. Snakes crack through dry oat weed, late sunlight honeying the hose water and the horses. Fields white as the sun sets. T makes sexual jokes over fresh cilantro and tortillas.

We are all sunburned, everyone but T, whose skin always looks like smooth chocolate, probably because he eats so much of it. (That is the Muhu Dojo motto: conserve energy to eat chocolate.)

I open the gate to the snaking dirt driveway. The moon looks like G-d's thumbnail. Insects whir like busy gears in some grand botanic clock.

三

I asked a therapist about self-defense at the end of my freshman year of high school. Cowering, be-braced, I wanted to be more confident in my own body. She knew Tautahcho. At home I called, nervous. His voice was even and friendly, but the first time I saw him he looked darkly over at me trembling at the edge of the mats and told me to sit in *seiza*, not like a lazy person. Years later, I look back and realize he was yanking my chain. At the time, I bought it.

One day Tautahcho saw a doodle I had drawn on my hand of a moon and a branch and drew a symbol on my other hand that told the story of the Chumash people's beginning. Every mark told a part of the story. It looked like a sun, spiked and layered.

One day the land was parched but foggy, and so T leaned outside the dojo window and howled and yipped. Sure enough, minutes later, it poured. In Southern California. In July. The rain just needed to be called.

Things I am good at:

With practice: *Shiko-ho*, the kneeling walk we use to traverse the mats without standing. When Tautahcho was feeling particular, he had us circle the mats four or five times instead of two. If the dojo had a partition, like it did during the years it was in the barn, he sent us in a pretzel loop that amused him and tired us.

Immediately: the *bokken*, the wooden practice sword. The first time Tauch ever bowed to me as I left the mats was after the session in which he surveyed me working with the sword for the first time and after twenty minutes said that I was a samurai. It is only this life that it is your first time, he said. One day he took down a sword with me and we did a two-man move round and round, up, out, sliding back, raise, pivot.

T uses the *bokken* of an old classmate of his, one who was amazing at sword work and who since suffered an injury that turned him into a vegetable. T says that on some level his friend gets to practice too.

On the mountain, Tautahcho made a leather bag. He cut the laces, told me that enlightenment meant being kind, Jesus and Buddha were the same spirit, and Jesus ("JC") died an old man in India—his "death" was really a breathing technique to stop his own heart that he learned on his travels. The house was small and made of adobe. Earthen mugs hung from nails on the rafters. Tautahcho's gnarled fingers worked with precision as he told me about Vietnam, partying in Saigon, working on the black market. I felt future and past blooming out of our bodies as fog moved, deliberate and bright, wrapping around the cob cottage: spider webs too small for our eyes, accustomed as they were to the conditions of the present, to see.

The morning before I met with the coyote I took the San Marcos Pass through rust-colored mountains to Santa Barbara for an MRI to check on the last four years of progress my unhappy spine had made. I had lived my first couple of months on a snow-covered campus and so paid extra attention to the green grasses and 80-degree weather of California January. I also knew to pay attention to the great fortune of health care because I had started to learn about that, too, in introductory social science courses. I remembered a promise I made to someone that I would never take the Pass because of its danger. I imagined my car teetering on the edge of the red cliff and me somehow go-go-gadgetting myself out the window as the car crashed down.

If the kids really realized what they have here on the mountain, T said emphatically of Betty's wayward teenagers that day as he knotted together strips of leather, they'd never leave.

Classic rock knows to come on when I drive up the mountain, and owls know to fly over me when I drive down it. One thing that tickles T is the assertion I made some years back that I was born in the wrong decade, the one without a living Hendrix. He likes that kind of music too, and listens to it out of a purple radio as he nails things together on his afternoons off from teaching.

One night Cassie was home from her father's and she and I fell to talking. She invited me on a walk. The moon was bright, the mountains silent. When we crawled under the gate and Cassie produced two cigarettes, I mentioned what I knew about Tauthcho giving his pot-smoking nephew twelve hours to get his stuff off of the mountain. Betty, one sunny day outside the only good coffee shop in the Santa Ynez Valley, told me how naïve she felt when she found out what T's nephew had been doing under their noses, how anyone who liked to "relax" was free to do so off of the mountain but never on, out of respect for T and how much he had overcome. Grass on the air, no one on the road. "Shit," said Cassie, "T used to be the biggest coke dealer in Santa Barbara."

Somewhere in the mountains children assembled alongside the elders. In front of them stood a group of junkies. There was chanting, and the elders blew on cups of plain water, and the water took on color. The junkies drank this and spent the next couple of days unable to move from their cots, vomiting, shitting uncontrollably, crying. What did the children do? someone asked. Cleaned up after us, man, said T. That was the most important part. Humbles you. Get all the disease and bad energy of drugs and alcohol out, and here is a child mopping up your puke. No ego after that.

We were all kneeling when T told us this. What did T puke? A loooot of alcohol. The fan was blowing. We quieted down, considering. Stretching time, we were mostly silent, but when T starts telling a story he gets on a roll pretty fast. We liked that, because some of the stretches were tame, like this one, done in sitting position, the *kote-gashi* lock we do on ourselves to ready our wrists in case someone does it to us.

五

Betty takes Levi and me, Choco the Labrador, and the cats, who heel, on a walk. Her slim body and ripe rump move easily in blue jeans. She points out flowers and names them, sits on a rock with her son in her lap, calling the cats, and when Pok the horse moves out from the group, it's Betty he follows and leans against, her yellow hair he noses. Later I am scooping lightly veined cantaloupe with a spoon when she calls me from behind the house, looking up at a sound, a hum, a hidden nest of bees. She wonders aloud how deep in its trunk the tree harbors the bees, lays a tan hand on the bark, puts her ear alongside it to listen. I feel a shock: this is why the present moment is important. I am the only human to see her sun-touched hair falling around her graceful profile, wide-open eyes like fresh water, her body at a slant with the tree, wholly listening.

I don't remember which of these presents is the one wherein Betty tells me about how, before they passed some years together in the same bed, T sometimes would wake up like lightning and grab her as if she were an enemy. It is the same conversation in which she says, by way of explanation, that he saw people blown up in Vietnam. The conversation in which she tells me the true story about someone being killed on their own front deck by a bullet fired up into the air miles away is a different one, one where we have leaning against the counter of the house with the oak tree outside the barn. One we have when I run into the kitchen and into her arms, crying, unable to sit there quietly and stretch because my father kicked me out of the car on the way to class after long minutes of shouting and driving too fast.

One of these present moments is one where T himself tells me about missile silos he's seen here in the mountains of California manned by guys whose job it is to mime blow-up time: open the red button box, stick their finger close to the red button, withdraw, close. Once every hour. T said, You should see those guys, all sleepy and stuff.

From the ranch on the mountain (formally Spirit Pine Ranch), I can see the ranch on which my high school is situated (Midland) and the ranch on which my childhood was situated (Highfield). A love triangle of my life, the lands from which, over years, love seeped into me, into my bones and innards, into my crowded head and crowded fears. The dogs pant and weave their paths together, rolling in thin pale dirt, sage sweet and thick on the air. Moths flutter among mustard weed and under hanging moss of thick-trunked oaks. Banks frozen into the shape of mudslides despite months without rain, and of course the prolific oat weed, bending. Countless more chipper throats in treetops. Goats murmur, leaning into my massage, their knobby spines secreting oil thickened with dust, the young ones with no more than stubs for horns.

When I went away, I visited the Mountain every time I came home. Each time I parked, as always, on Figueroa Mountain, the road leading past Midland and, upward miles later, past Spirit Pine, so I could walk in. Walk in and breathe out whatever I accumulated elsewhere, where purity is less obvious, less omnipresent. I breathed out hung-over mornings and frightening looks from strange men in cities far from here, breathed out imagining it all dissolving into the swept landscape. Red rock, yucca. Here I am, again. Slate, gopher holes.

Every time I returned, something new: the first floor of Cassie's cob house built, a garden taking shape, a trough repaired.

One visit: at first it seems deserted, and that is just as well. I cuddle with the sweet new dog, Byron, and look around, thinking, Thank you universe once again for delivering me from the deep. Out to this, the Mountain, my destination. I wonder if maybe I should knock on the door. Then I hear Levi cough from his bedroom, think maybe they're all napping.

I hear the sound of a garden tool being used, wander around the side of the house and see someone toiling away by the "stool shed." The person is blonde. I think maybe Betty. But it is a slim, dirt-covered man. I say hello. We introduce. He is Michael. Come to do work and live close to nature, as do many friends of Betty and T, as have I. He is a carpenter and earning his keep. I find, and have tea and soup with, Betty. The soup is amazing, just what I wanted. Betty is always cooking just what I want. Or her mother, Gradnma Jackie, is baking just what I want.

One day in early summer there were strings and strings of sage hanging in scraggly grins to dry in bunches. Betty gave me some to take to school. Even now it lies in a jeweled dish in my dorm room, and I burn it when I need to.

六

Of the coyote day I have nothing to say but what I wrote about it, almost nothing to remember but what I wrote about it. I cannot tell now as I read the letter I sent to friends and family about it whether I would remember the things I wrote in the letter if I had not written the letter, if I would remember, for instance, the car—a wild animal, swerving of its own accord, if I would remember the lonely sound of my scream as the windshield acquiesced to a branch in the dark and erupted into a cobweb of fractures.

I wrote all this down, and so I glean that it happened, I wrote all this down and so it happens again. A couple of hours after I kiss the earth outside of Tautahcho's house, I swerve in my father's car to avoid hitting a large coyote and the car spins out of control, runs off the road, flips at least once, maybe three times, and lands upside down in the median in between a large culvert and a large tree. When I see the huge branch of oak lit by headlights come crashing towards me, I think now I will know what it is to be injured or how it is to die. I think the car is an animal, and I cannot get out, cannot stop the car, cannot stop screaming.

The radio is still playing the Beatles when the rest has quieted—"I know this love of mine/ Will never die"—as I squirm, upside down, out of my seat belt and crawl through the window. All of the side windows blown out. I am the only one in the car and on that stretch of Highway 101 that night. The singular sound of my footsteps as I jog across the road, unscratched, fills the air along with the light of an almost-full moon.

Earlier, on the way back from Santa Barbara, I took the highway to see the ocean spread out at the foot of a flushed rose sunset. Mountains cozied up to the coastline, pale rocky faces striped with dark vegetation. Before going home, I visited Tautahcho and his family on the Mountain. We stood and witnessed the very last of the day together, red light stretching along the horizon, eating yams cooked in the adobe oven and making plans for me to stay with them over the summer to practice Aikido and help them build their cob house. Stars were out by the time I left, winking over sagebrush, and I was so taken with sudden reverence at this beautiful patch of the planet and the loving people on it that, after checking that no one could see me, I knelt and kissed the red dirt.

Not much time passed between then and that moment, between then and the coyote scampering, scared and pale, out in front of the car: my own scream when the car seems to lose its mind, coyote's bright green eyes locking with mine, dewy grasses against my arm as the car rolls, that Beatles song hanging in the air the first moment I would be dead: "Bright are the stars that shine…"

"Even now," I wrote, "I startle myself awake at the urgent memory of the coyote, of myself breathing 'thank you' to a nearly round moon as the oaks stand in silent testimony. I wait for my bruises to fade. I live a life I might not have lived, and it is not a life in which I choose to be ashamed or apologetic of wonder, of the power of reverence of land and people to protect me."

My parents were grateful that they knew I was all right before seeing the car, upside-down, smashed, windows blown out, oil leaking onto long grass whitened by moonlight. I write of beauty to strain out the huge pain of alarm, the huge movement I could not control, the huge sound. I try to choose what remains.

I called T the next day and left a message about the accident. I knew he knows about coyotes. He called up immediately and called me sweetie. I said, Tauch, what does it mean? He said, The coyote was running from your right to your left, close to your turnoff on 101? Yes. It was running south, towards the darkness. Let the darkness in. Don't run, don't fear it.

But you know what? Mostly, he wants you to slow down. Take time. Look around. He was telling you to slow down.

Awkward corporeal grace occupying us like a virus, our shoulders like violins.

We live lives we might not have lived, even when we cannot hear the singing, cannot hear the screaming.

Sage secretes its heady spice across a purpling sky, voices of critters a low hum. Tautahcho tells me that to walk the earth is to soak its love and energy through your feet, to walk in forest is to consult your elders. The intense heat and dust of summer, the slick head of a baby goat bulging out of its groaning mother. The night, the stars, the hay, the barn. This I know: the land loves me back.

My father spent the whole next day with me, bought me my favorite chocolate cupcakes and sat with me while I ate them, said he would have made an anthology of my writing for all the world to see.

The moments are rare, when you truly feel something before it is gone, before you don't have it anymore. When I fly home I will again walk over dirt, I will again kiss. Planet and people both.

I think if my core were visible it would look like sun-drenched oak trees. Red rock, yucca.

ACKNOWLEDGMENTS

I owe a great and heartfelt debt to the editors at those publications who gave print to a few of the pieces in this manuscript: *Arts & Letters* for publishing "Lenin" as the finalist for the Susan Atefat Prize in Creative Nonfiction; *Caper Journal* for publishing an earlier version of "Furious Angels" back when it was called "The Poem That Still Speaks:" *The Chattahoochee Review* for publishing "Coyote" as the winner of the Lamar York Nonfiction Prize; *Crab Orchard Review* for publishing much of "The Surest Way To Survive" as the Honorable Mention in the John Guyon Literary Nonfiction Prize; *Hayden's Ferry Review* for publishing "Jacqueline and the Negative Imagination:" and *The Poker* for publishing "Typewriter." Thanks also to the folks at *Best American Essays 2015* and *Best American Essays 2016*, which named "Lenin" and "Jacqueline and the Negative Imagination," respectively, Notable Essays.

Through Wolfram Productions, Charlotte Austin and Siolo Thompson supported the Survival Girls early and often. So did the incomparable artist Jody Joldersma, and actors Michael Littig and Julianna Bloodgood. Nita and Justin Davanzo of DogStar Theater Company gave me wings as an actor to explore what the Survival Girls taught me. My adviser Stephanie Batiste created spaces within which I could both write and act about it all, bridging the critical and creative self. Rick Benjamin saw me clearly, saw me often for grilled cheeses, and saw me through my PhD exam summer by giving "dramatic readings" of my theory texts. We came by it honestly, Rick.

As I grew up, my other mentors did right by me and then some: Catherine Imbriglio, Honor Moore, Forrest Gander, Robert and Pen Creeley, Thalia Field, Brian Evenson, Noy Holland, Linda Oppen, Ian and Lynda Cummings, Derek Svennungsen, David and Karen Jensen, Cynthia Carbone Ward, Shawn and Laura McVicar, Tautahcho Muhuawit and Betty Seaman, Ross Gay, Samrat Upadhyay, Alex Halberstadt, Catherine Bowman, Jill Schoolman, Mark Minton, Stacey Harwood, Jacinda Townsend, Leslie Jamison, Li Ling, Perie Longo, Fanny Howe, Joseph Roberts, Kate Vrijmoet, Teresa Vargas Alvarez and the rest of the Quito family, Nadezhda and

Anatoly, Erdentuya Khaadbaatar, Bill and Betina Infante, and my third-grade teacher, Lynn Rector, who informed my parents when I was eight years old that they had a writer.

My cohort, in class and in life, kept me inspired: Bronwen Tate, Rachel L'Abri Tipton, Emily Underwood, Katherine Goldstein, Anat Mooreville, Rachel Lyon, Brian Christian, Cecil Sayre, Andrew Marantz, Stacey Petrek, Lila Fischer, Alexandra Kleeman, Selena Hsu, Michael Solis, Lauren Neal, Jenny Zhang, Mel Grunow, Rena Heinrich, Luke Meinzen, Sara Taylor, Cheri Mayhugh, Anja Tranovich, Lesley Carmichael, Renee Nixon, Gabriel Williams, Mal Hellman, Sos Bagramyan.

Taylor Brown, thank you for giving me an experience.

My parents prioritized helping me get to school and for that I am immensely grateful. I was partly raised by the good people who work at a lot of marvelous institutions: The Family School, Midland School, Vassar College, Brown University's Literary Arts Department, Indiana University's MFA in Creative Writing, UCSB's department of Theater and Dance as well as its Interdisciplinary Humanities Center, the Santa Barbara Foundation, the Henry Luce Foundation, the Wesleyan Writers Conference, the Juniper Summer Writing Institute, the Disquiet Literary Conference, the Summer Literary Seminars, and the Santa Barbara Writers Conference. I was given room to grow into myself—a room of my own, you might say—through the recognition and freedom of the Henry Luce Scholars Program, Indiana University's Herman B. Wells Graduate Fellowship, and the University of California's Regents Special Fellowship. Summer adventures in international development are owed to Brown University's Michael Harper Poetry Service Assistantship, the Kim Ann Artstark Award, the Kapstein Premium, and the Assatly Award for Praxis; the Santa Barbara Foundation's Pillsbury Award for Creative Writing; the *Glimmer Train* Family Matters Award; and Indiana University's Woon-Joon Yoon Memorial Fellowship and International Enhancement grant (which in particular led to my work with the Survival Girls group). Professional training and partnership is a commitment especially to the people in positions to teach me, and in addition to the mentors responsible for my schooling, I owe a great deal to the good folks at the UNHCR, GTZ, Karam Founation, the Rio Beni Health Foundation, the

Asia Foundation, Archipelago Books, and People Helping People.

If there's anything good about me or this book, my family is largely responsible for it, particularly my mom, Miki, who edited early versions of this manuscript and also earlier versions of me, and my dad, David, who sang silly songs and made pesto pasta for me to gobble up while reading and writing at the dining room table since I was in grade school. Thank you to all the Holdens and McCaslins, Hochfeldts and Cooleys, Austins and Esveldts, near and far, for getting me there.

Lisa Bowden, Ann Dernier, and Lidia Yuknavitch all made sure this book saw the light of day, after I'd spent thirteen years working on it and hoping. Thank you for your patience with me, Kore Press!

Matt: there you are.

The subjects of these essays are some of the people I love best in the world, who have taught me the most, to whom I owe the very greatest thanks. This book is for them, toward them, as a small token of their immense gifts to me of time, presence, hospitality, and trust. Even when their names are changed, they know who they are, and they are always why.

NOTES

Almost all the names and specifically identifying circumstances in this book have been changed. Exceptions include those refugees who asked to keep their real names in this book, and a few doctors in South America whose work deserves awareness.

Whether or not names were changed, those whom I could track down have received news of this book, and in most cases copies of the essay. However, standards of journalistic rigor don't apply easily to situations wherein I was listening to one person describe their past struggles. I did not approach these stories the way a journalist is trained to do, and search out a second source to confirm any details: confirmation of fact was never as important to me as fidelity to the act of listening to someone, and giving the power of the truth to them. Any mistakes in the representation of the people in this book are on my shoulders, and mine alone.

THE SUREST WAY TO SURVIVE:
The epigraph for the third section of this essay is the first line of Barbara Kingsolver's book *The Poisonwood Bible*.

I misunderstood the note from Abu Faisal: it was Abu Mahrouz, the commander brother of Dr. Mahrouz, who was captured by ISIS, not the doctor himself. Abu Mahrouz headed what's called "The 5th Corps," an amalgamation of five FSA squads, at the request of the US government. The commander, whose children are even younger than his brother the doctor's, was released a few days later. He was killed by ISIS in 2017.

Writes Abu Faisal: " They stopped his entourage at a checkpoint and tried to kill him. They killed one of his lieutenants and he managed to escape. Abu Mahrous and his Free Idlib Army are the last group left in Idleb to counter Al Qaida and the Assad regime and they're getting almost no support. But that's the usual! As for our projects and aid work, it's a disaster (in Syria) and going well (in Turkey). Everything we've ever built in Syria has been destroyed twice. Really, twice. We build it, Assad bombs it. We build it again. He bombs it again. Every school and every hospital is gone."

For those who might be moved to donate to the cause: the Karam Foundation does wonderful work for Syrians everywhere.

WHAT YOU WAIT FOR:
Ever a quick study, Ahmad finished formal study of the Swedish language and awaits a place at university in Sweden. He was also joined in Sweden by his fiancé in 2016. As of November 2017, they were awaiting their first child, Zaid, due in January 2018. Writes Ahmad: "I can't describe how I feel when we buy Zaid's clothes … Two hearts now I have… one of it is for Zaid!"

TYPEWRITER:
George Oppen (April 24, 1908-July 7, 1984) won the Pulitzer Prize for poetry in 1969. A member of the Objectivist group of poets, he spent around two decades in Mexico after his

political activism (for which he abandoned his poetry for several years) led him to be a person of interest to the House Un-American Activities Committee.

George's handwriting is lively—his notes are scribbled over each other in faded pencil and pen, with some things crossed out, and exclamation marks here and there. He also had some things to say about Aeschylus 1 in the margins: "Crime," "murder," "Symbol," etc. I guess Mary had been the one to take pencil to Adams' *The United States in 1800*, as the underlines were clean and straight and the letters well-formed.

The handwriting of the poem I found on a yellow notepad probably *is* Mary's, but the poem is not. The poem turns out to have been an early draft of "Poem of Myself" by Rachel Blau DuPlessis, sent from the author, who was staying in France, to the Oppens on Eagle for editing/suggestions. Sincere apologies to DuPlessis, who responded gracefully to not having been known, and therefore cited, as the true author in the earliest draft of this piece. "Poem of Myself" in its final form can be found in DuPlessis' book *Wells*, published in 1980 by the Montemora Foundation. Gratitude also to DuPlessis for allowing the above earlier version of her poem to remain here.

JACQUELINE AND THE NEGATIVE IMAGINATION:

p. 124: "The Survivor Girls of Congo" https://www.youtube.com/watch?v=gR-KX0XS9LU, posted 11/9/12

Bibliography of work quoted in this essay:

Anna Deveare Smith, *Four American Characters*, TED Talk web video, 23:05, February 2005, https://www.ted.com/talks/anna_deavere_smith_s_american_character.

Carruth, Cathy, editor. "Trauma: Explorations in Memory." Johns Hopkins University Press. 1995.

Chung, Anna Anlin. "Melancholy of Race." *Kenyon Review*, Vol. 19, no. 1 (1997): 49-61.

Gallagher, Shaun. *How The Body Shapes The Mind*. Oxford: Oxford University Press (2005). Print

Grosz, Elizabeth. *Volatile Bodies: Toward a Corporeal Feminism*. USA: Allen & Unwin (1994). Print.

Halberstam and Livingston, eds. *Posthuman Bodies (Unnatural Acts: Theorizing the Performative)*. USA: Indiana University Press (1995). Print.

Kubiak, Anthony. "Splitting the Difference: Performance and its Double in American Culture." *TDR* 42, no. 4 (Winter 1998): 91-114.

FURIOUS ANGELS: THE POETICS OF POLITICAL EXILE:

The sections of this essay are named according to "One," "Two," Three," etc in Mongolian, using the Cyrillic alphabet.

The found poem in italics featured throughout this essay is wrought from these works:

James Agee and Walker Evans, *Let Us Now Praise Famous Men*

Samuel Beckett, *Waiting for Godot*

William Blake, *The Marriage of Heaven and Hell*

Charlotte Brontë, *Jane Eyre*

Emily Dickinson, *Collected Poems*

William Faulkner, *Light in August*

Forrest Gander, *Torn Awake*

Toni Morrison, *Beloved*

Abbé Prévost, *Manon Lescaut*

Adrienne Rich, *The Fact of a Doorframe*

William Shakespeare, *Othello*

Sophocles, *Oedipus Rex*

Walt Whitman, *Leaves of Grass*

Attribution by line:

PAGE 141:

Where a flat-sided steep frowns over the present world, / William Blake, *The Marriage of
        Heaven and Hell*

My elbows rest in sea-gaps / Walt Whitman, *Leaves of Grass*

Of orbic tendencies to shape and shape and shape / Whitman, *Leaves of Grass*

PAGE 142:

The body lurking there within thy body, / Whitman, *Leaves of Grass*

Carrying even her moonsails. / Whitman, *Leaves of Grass*

The sea is not a question of power. / Adrienne Rich, "Diving Into The Wreck"

Those clarities detached us, gave us form. / Rich, "Diving Into The Wreck"

Hungry clouds swag on the deep, / Blake, *The Marriage of Heaven and Hell*

The chief inlets of soul in this age. / Blake, *The Marriage of Heaven and Hell*

PAGE 143:

The driver asked us where he was to go. / Antoine Francois (Abbé) Prévost, *Manon Lescaut*

'To the end of the world!' I cried. / Prévost, *Manon Lescaut*

When I came home, on the abyss of the five senses, / Blake, *The Marriage of Heaven and Hell*

The placenta of the real, / Rich, "The Phenomenology of Anger"

boundless as a nether sky / Blake, *The Marriage of Heaven and Hell*

Into the deep, down falling, even to eternity down falling, / Blake, *The Marriage of Heaven
        and Hell*

The hoary element roaring— / Blake, *The Marriage of Heaven and Hell*

I have to learn alone / Rich, "Diving Into The Wreck"

To turn my body without force in the deep element / Rich, "Diving Into The Wreck"

PAGE 144:

With that inward listening deliberation / William Faulkner, *Light in August*

The thirst-perishing man might feel / Charlotte Brontë, *Jane Eyre*

Who knows the well to which he has crept is poisoned / Brontë, *Jane Eyre*

Lowering himself from rung to rung in onehanded swoops, / Faulkner, *Light In August*

The bone hands roped with vein. / James Agee, *Let Us Now Praise Famous Men*

Seen in the smoke of cannon as in a vision / Faulkner, *Light in August*

That the laying on of hands meant literally that. / Faulkner, *Light in August*

'Everything in life seems unreal.' / Brontë, *Jane Eyre*

'Except me: I am substantial enough—touch me.' / Brontë, *Jane Eyre*

'You, sir, are the most phantom-like of all: you are a mere dream.' / Brontë, *Jane Eyre*

He held out his hand, laughing. / Brontë, *Jane Eyre*

'Is that a dream?' said he, placing it close to my eyes. I have heard of day-dreams-is she in a
    day-dream now? / Brontë, *Jane Eyre*

Her eyes are fixed on the floor, but I am sure / Brontë, *Jane Eyre*

They do not see it—her sight seems turned in, / Brontë, *Jane Eyre*

Gone down into her heart: she is looking / Brontë, *Jane Eyre*

At what she can remember, I believe; / Brontë, *Jane Eyre*

Not at what is really present. / Brontë, *Jane Eyre*

And on the bleached bones / Blake, *The Marriage of Heaven and Hell*

You listened to the sobbing wind. / Brontë, *Jane Eyre*

Watch out for her; she can give you dreams / Toni Morrison, *Beloved*

Whatever place she run from ain't going to be a whole lot / Faulkner, *Light in August*

Different or worse than the place she is at. / Faulkner, *Light in August*

We dream—it is good we are dreaming- / Dickinson, poem #531

It would hurt us-were we awake. / Dickinson, poem #531

That son grew to manhood among phantoms, / Faulkner, *Light in August*

And side by side with a ghost, puddled his clear spirit, / Shakespeare, *Othello*

Then leaped into the void between saturn and the fixed stars— / Blake, *The Marriage of Heaven
    and Hell*

That silence wherein more deep than starlight this home is foundered / Agee, *Let Us Now
    Praise Famous Men*

Behold him, part wakened, fallen among field flowers shallow / Agee, *Let Us Now
    Praise Famous Men*

But undisclosed, withdraw. Time had stopped there and then for the seed / Agee, *Let Us Now
    Praise Famous Men*

And nothing had happened in time since, not even him. / Agee, *Let Us Now Praise Famous Men*

He caused the inside of the cave to be infinite. / Blake, *The Marriage of Heaven and Hell*

Or is it that in starry places we see things we long to see? / Rich, "For The Conjunction
    of Two Planets"

Let me die by inches. / Sophocles, *Oedipus Rex*

The sword was suspended above our heads by a single thread which was about to snap.
    / Prévost, *Manon Lescaut*

Lift her head from the depths, the red waves of death / Sophocles, *Oedipus Rex*

As though it were a ghost traveling a half mile ahead of its own shape. / Faulkner,
    Light in August

I have wept through nights, you must know that, / Sophocles, *Oedipus Rex*
Groping laboring over many paths of thought. / Sophocles, *Oedipus Rex*

PAGE 150:

The water is brilliant and nervy, / Agee, *Let Us Now Praise Famous Men*
Breaking up by her entrance / Brontë, *Jane Eyre*
the fiery mosaic I had been piecing together. / Brontë, *Jane Eyre*
Lest the Phantasm-prove the Mistake— / Dickinson, poem # 531
that you can fully appreciate all the circumstances of our ruin I must elucidate its cause:
        / Prévost, *Manon Lescaut*
A furious angel nailed to the ground by his wings. / Agee, *Let Us Now Praise Famous Men*
That called body is a portion of soul / Blake, *The Marriage of Heaven and Hell*
Which cast the metals into the expanse / Blake, *The Marriage of Heaven and Hell*
To gaze at anagrams of light. / Rich, "For The Conjunction of Two Planets"

PAGE 151:

The imaginary whistle blows / Faulkner, *Light in August*
Out on this stony planet that we farm / Rich, *Stepping Backward*
making the familiar faces of men appear strange, / Faulkner, *Light in August*
and every One unbared a Nerve: / Dickinson, poem *#479*
the wondrous fivewindowed nerve and core. The fat gold fly who sang and botched against a
        bright pane within. / Agee, *Let Us Now Praise Famous Men*
She opens the grass. / Morrison, *Beloved*
There's no lack of void. / Beckett, *Waiting for Godot*
The sweetness of your face is just another threat. / Prévost, *Manon Lescaut*
I don't know who we thought we were. / Rich, "From A Survivor"

PAGE 152:

But did that ever happen to us? / Beckett, *Waiting for Godot*

PAGE 153:

All the dead voices. / Beckett, *Waiting for Godot*
They make a noise like wings. / Beckett, *Waiting for Godot*
Like leaves. / Beckett, *Waiting for Godot*
Like sand. / Beckett, *Waiting for Godot*
Like leaves. / Beckett, *Waiting for Godot*

PAGE 154:

My greatest hobby was making little chapels / Prévost, *Manon Lescaut*
Run like quicksilver wheat in the lesions of heated air / Agee, *Let Us Now Praise Famous Men*
Out there where that house is burning, / Faulkner, *Light in August*
The bells bruising the air above the crowded roofs. / Rich, "The Tourist and the Town"
The houses are broken open like pods in the increase of the sun, / Agee, *Let Us Now
        Praise Famous Men*
and they are scattered on the wind of a day's work, / Agee, *Let Us Now Praise Famous Men*
alive and separate in that bell-struck air. / Rich, "The Celebration in the Plaza"
'And what is hell? Can you tell me that?' / Brontë, *Jane Eyre*

The fading fires just showed her coming up the long, vacant room / Brontë, *Jane Eyre*

as though out of some trivial and unimportant region beyond even distance. / Faulkner,
  Light In August

I was in a printing-house in Hell / Blake, *The Marriage of Heaven and Hell*

and saw the method with which knowledge / Blake, *The Marriage of Heaven and Hell*

was transmitted from generation to generation, / Blake, *The Marriage of Heaven and Hell*

from his cold-house secret / Morrison, *Beloved*

straight to her too-thick love. / Morrison, *Beloved*

Each is a new and incommunicably tender life, wounded with every breath. / Agee, *Let Us Now
  Praise Famous Men*

The human act will make us real again. / Rich, "Stepping Backward"

I tried to make my eyes blaze with other fires than those of love, / Prévost, *Manon Lescaut*

With corroding fires, / Blake, *The Marriage of Heaven and Hell*

or whistle's echo, sinking, sunken. / Agee, *Let Us Now Praise Famous Men*

Tell him… tell him you saw me and that… that you saw me. / Beckett, *Waiting for Godot*

You have rather the look / Brontë, *Jane Eyre*

of another world. / Brontë, *Jane Eyre*

We have our reasons. / Beckett, *Waiting for Godot*

How could you leave the crime uncleansed so long? / Sophocles, *Oedipus Rex*

You cannot explain to others because they have no conception of what is meant. / Prévost,
  Manon Lescaut

They say they are ions in the sun. / Rich, "August"

You may say it is to prevent our reason from foundering. / Beckett, *Waiting for Godot*

Look the house in its blind face. / Agee, *Let Us Now Praise Famous Men*

the Film upon the eye / Dickinson, Poem #479

had the opal lightings of dark oil. / Agee, *Let Us Now Praise Famous Men*

Winging, swept away, / Sophocles, *Oedipus Rex*

What good were eyes to me? / Sophocles, *Oedipus Rex*

The words are purposes. / Rich, "Diving Into The Wreck"

The words are maps. / Rich, "Diving Into The Wreck"

I myself but write one or two indicative words for the future. / Whitman, *Leaves of Grass*

She persuaded us to let the mystery go / Sophocles, *Oedipus Rex*

And concentrate on what lay at our feet. / Sophocles, *Oedipus Rex*

The worst of words. / Shakespeare, *Othello*

The original quarry, abyss itself. / Faulkner, *Light In August*

You need riches, armies to bring that quarry down! / Sophocles, *Oedipus Rex*

Will you swallow, will you deny them, will you lie your way home? / Rich, "Rape"
It is weak and silly to say you cannot bear what it is your fate to be required to bear. /
    Brontë, *Jane Eyre*

PAGE 161:
You have not wept at all! / Brontë, *Jane Eyre*
I see a white cheek and a faded eye, / Brontë, *Jane Eyre*
But no trace of tears. I suppose, then, / Brontë, Jane Eyre
Your heart has been weeping blood? / Brontë, Jane Eyre
I have always stood in the way of your pleasures. / Prévost, *Manon Lescaut*
Open your eyes. Look and see who I am. / Prévost, *Manon Lescaut*
Witness, you ever- / Shakespeare, *Othello*
burning lights above, who are so lovely / Shakespeare, *Othello*
fair and smellst so sweet / Shakespeare, *Othello*
that the sense aches at thee: / Shakespeare, *Othello*
Suppose we repented. / Beckett, *Waiting for Godot*

PAGE 162:
Give me the ocular proof, / Shakespeare, *Othello*
if only to save you from freezing at the street corner all night, / Prévost, *Manon Lescaut*
to comply with heat: / Shakespeare, *Othello*
Bells in your parlors, wildcats in your kitchens; / Shakespeare, *Othello*
After every tempest come such calms. / Shakespeare, *Othello*
Even then this forked plague is fated to us. / Shakespeare, *Othello*

PAGE 163:
Repented what? / Beckett, *Waiting for Godot*
Our being born? / Beckett, *Waiting for Godot*
Remorse is the poison of life. / Brontë, *Jane Eyre*

PAGE 164:
What if /Forrest Gander, "The Hugeness of That Which is Missing"
a man went into his house and leaned his hand / Gander,
    "The Hugeness of That Which is Missing"
against the wall and the wall / Gander, "The Hugeness of That Which is Missing"
was not? / Gander, "The Hugeness of That Which is Missing"

PAGE 165:
Better than any description of buildings or garments, / Blake, *The Marriage of Heaven and Hell*
The theory of a city, a poem, / Whitman, *Leaves of Grass*
With iron and stone edifices, ceaseless vehicles, / Whitman, *Leaves of Grass*
As a matter of decent of form rather than rebellion— / Agee, *Let Us Now Praise Famous Men*
Formed a heaven of what he stole from the abyss. / Blake, *The Marriage of Heaven and Hell*
Ship and towered city are nothing, / Sophocles, *Oedipus Rex*
Stripped of men alive within it, living as one. / Sophocles, *Oedipus Rex*

PAGE 166:

Picking out our way through verbs and ruins, / Rich, *The Tourist and the Town*

That single idle word blown from mind to mind. / Faulkner, *Light in August*

His blood began again, talking and talking. / Faulkner, *Light in August*

Did the letters work upon his blood? / Shakespeare, *Othello*

The breastlike, floral air is / Agee, *Let Us Now Praise Famous Men*

the bloody tribute we had paid that harsh, brutal singer / Sophocles, *Oedipus Rex*

at the deadest hours of the night. / Brontë, *Jane Eyre*

At each stroke blood spurts from the roots. / Sophocles, *Oedipus Rex*

PAGE 167:

Eyes going and going, / Faulkner, *Light in August*

A swirl of it, nerves and clots, / Sophocles, *Oedipus Rex*

Can roar in the heart of itself as a symphony, / Agee, *Let Us Now Praise Famous Men*

Perhaps as no symphony can. / Agee, *Let Us Now Praise Famous Men*

Whatever is neglected slips away. / Sophocles, *Oedipus Rex*

You elements that clip us round about, / Shakespeare, *Othello*

All sent back by the echoes: / Whitman, *Leaves of Grass*

Heaven has always chosen the time. / Prévost, *Manon Lescaut*

PAGE 168:

All times mischoose. / Whitman, *Leaves of Grass*

The boss was dead, the mistress nervous and the cradle already split. / Morrison, *Beloved*

I did what human beings do instinctively when / Brontë, *Jane Eyre*

They are driven to utter extremity—looked / Brontë, *Jane Eyre*

For aid to one higher than man. / Brontë, *Jane Eyre*

PAGE 169:

Is reform needed? / Whitman, *Leaves of Grass*

Is it through you? / Whitman, *Leaves of Grass*

No message plucked from the birds, the embers. / Sophocles, *Oedipus Rex*

Always a knit of identity, / Whitman, *Leaves of Grass*

The moon had opened a blue field in the sky. / Brontë, *Jane Eyre*

Where's my voice? / Sophocles, *Oedipus Rex*

Where are all these corpses from, / Beckett, *Waiting For Godot*

Scattering too some heavy / Brontë, *Jane Eyre*

Unwelcome thoughts that were beginning to throng on my solitude? / Brontë, *Jane Eyre*

PAGE 170:

What do you do / Beckett, *Waiting For Godot*

when you fall far from help? / Beckett, *Waiting For Godot*

Night doesn't fall. / Beckett, *Waiting For Godot*

Left to myself I abandoned myself: / Brontë, *Jane Eyre*

I think the sun where he was born drew all such humours from him, / Shakespeare, *Othello*

For he only holds a candle in the sunshine. / Blake, *The Marriage of Heaven and Hell*

The thing I came for: the wreck / Rich, "Diving Into the Wreck"

243

and not the story of the wreck. / Rich, "Diving Into the Wreck"
You won't hear it nicely. If it hurts you, be glad of it. / Agee, *Let Us Now Praise Famous Men*

PAGE 171:
It is very late in the day to offer me your tears. / Prévost, *Manon Lescaut*
Now about setting you free: / Prévost, *Manon Lescaut*
I cannot fall because there is no room to. / Morrison, *Beloved*
Rescue yourself, your city, rescue me— / Sophocles, *Oedipus Rex*
Rescue everything infected by the dead. / Sophocles, *Oedipus Rex*

PAGE 172:
How can I say things that are pictures: / Morrison, *Beloved*
To say: be kinder to yourself. / Rich, "For The Dead"
The earth abode of stones in the great deeps, / Beckett, *Waiting for Godot*
the only name I have for you, that, no other—ever, ever, ever! / Sophocles, *Oedipus Rex*

PAGE 173:
In rooms of selfhood where we woke and lay watching / Rich, "Ideal Landscape"
today unfold like yesterday, we had to take the world / Rich, "Ideal Landscape"
as it was given. / Rich, "Ideal Landscape"
The human rose to haunt us / Rich, "Ideal Landscape"
everywhere, raw, flawed, and asking more than we could bear. / Rich, "Ideal Landscape"
(How was it we were caught?) / Agee, *Let Us Now Praise Famous Men*

Tumenulzii came to the U.S.A. in 2011, where a Human Rights Watch Hellman-Hammett grant of $5,000 awaited him. Because I was the one who nominated him for the grant, Tumenulzii insisted on using some of it to help me get a new laptop; when I visited him and his daughter at their house in Brooklyn in 2012, he shook his head and laughed at the heavy, Gobi-soil-smeared laptop I'd been working on ever since we met in 2007. I type this now on a little laptop I wouldn't have been able to get without him. His daughter earned a degree from the New School, and his wife joined them in 2013. Tumenulzii and his wife walk for forty-five minutes every morning around their neighborhood in Brighton Beach.

SICKNESS:
The Rio Beni Health Project is now a Bolivian entity, the Rio Beni Health Foundation. Chris Brady invites you to email him and start a conversation if you're interested in donating: CBrady.RB@gmail.com

COYOTE:
Section headings are the numbers "One," "Two," Three," etc in Japanese.

ABOUT THE AUTHOR

Author photo by Shyn Midili

Ming Lauren Holden is an activist, actor, educator and writer who was raised on a zebra ranch on California's central coast. Ming has worked in the international development sector on four continents in thirteen countries since 2001. She founded the Survival Girls, a self-sustaining theater group for Congolese refugee women in a Nairobi slum, a project that received support from then-Secretary of State Hillary Clinton. Ming studied Literary Arts at Brown University; earned her MFA at Indiana University; and is currently pursuing a PhD in Theater and Dance at the University of California, Santa Barbara, where she teaches undergraduates and incarcerated youth and researches how theater can help with rehabilitation and trauma recovery.

ABOUT THE PRESS

 As a community of literary activists devoted to bringing forth a diversity of voices through works that meet the highest artistic standards, Kore Press publishes women's writing that deepens awareness and advances progressive social change.

Kore has been publishing the creative genius of women since 1993 in Tucson, to ensure more equitable public discourse and take action toward establishing a more inclusive, democratic, and accurate historic record.

- Since its inception in 1923, *Time Magazine* has had one female editor.

- Since 1948, the Pulitzer Prize for Poetry has gone to 51 men and 19 women.

- Only twelve of 109 Nobel Prizes for Literature have gone to women. Three of the twelve female winners were in the last decade.

Become a literary activist and support feminist, independent publishing by purchasing books directly from the publisher, by making a tax-deductible contribution to Kore, or becoming a member of the Press. Please visit us at korepress.org.